FOR *Love* AND TREASURE

Books by Monty Joynes

Naked Into the Night (1997)

Lost In Las Vegas (1998)

Save the Good Seed (1999)

Dead Water Rites (2000)

The Celestine Prophecy: The Making of the Movie (2005)

Conversations With God: The Making of the Movie (2006)

*Journey For The One: The Biography of
Jeanne White Eagle and John Pehrson* (2008)

GRID (2011)

Flesh (2011)

Psalm Maker: The Journal of Booker Jones (2013)

*Confessions of a Channeler: A Reluctant
Man's Journey Into Mysticism* (2014)

FOR  *Love* AND TREASURE

The Life and Times of the
World's Most Successful
Treasure Hunting Family

MONTY JOYNES

SEASIDE BOOKS

Cover and interior design by Frame25 Productions
Cover photo © Mel Fisher's Treasures

Published by:
Seaside Books
44 Seaside South Court
Key West, Fl 33040

If you are unable to order this book from your local
bookseller, you may order directly from the distributor.

Square One Publishers, Inc.
115 Herricks Road
Garden City Park, NY 11040
Phone: (516) 535-2010
Fax: (516) 535-2014
Toll-free: 877-900-BOOK

Visit the author at:
www.montyjoynes.com

Library of Congress Cataloging-in-Publication Data applied for.
ISBN 978-0-692-39931-6

10 9 8 7 6 5 4 3 2 1

Printed on acid-free paper in Canada

Acknowledgments

A biographer coming into a long established family-centered company as the new guy from out of town wonders if he will be accepted. Then the stranger begins to poke around into the lives of people who know each other well. Even introductions made in good faith do not ensure cooperation, let alone trust. Yet, despite my intrusions and persistent questioning, the Fisher family and its company staff not only embraced me, but they also extended to me great kindness and generosity. To name them individually would necessitate reproducing the company staff roster to which would be added the names of expedition members, Fisher family friends, and the new social pals who showed me around the character of Key West.

Those who know me in the literary trade recognize that my wife Pat comprises my entire support system as editor and managing partner. I could not be away from home for months of research and complete a book manuscript on deadline without her dedicated efforts.

To everyone associated with the Fisher family enterprises, I am very grateful to be your biographer. I dedicated myself to tell your story with a great deal of enthusiasm and respect. I trust that this book will honor all of you and add to your legacy as the greatest shipwreck treasure finders, salvors, and conservators in world history. I am very proud to know you and to consider you my friends for life.

Contents

Introduction

We are explorers in the depths of a salt sea even though we emerged from that brine a million years ago. We cannot hold our breath too long under water, and our vision is limited to a few feet around a circumference of suspicious shadows. The depth pressure on our ears must be compensated, and even then the sounds vibrating through the translucent liquid are reminiscent of distant echoes. Be prepared when you venture below the surface of even a calm sea that you are no primal match for the denizens who regard you as an oddly propelled interloper.

Human men and women who dare to hunt and salvage in oceanic planes must adjust to a water world of wonders that will distract them by fascination and thus blind them to its siren dangers. And yet, the call of the sea's deep mysteries beckons some to a lifetime of experimental devotion. Its secrets entrance them, and they must slip beneath the waves of surface circumstances to encounter an alternative reality. The rest of us must vicariously follow them and pretend that we have been where they have been and seen what they have seen.

Our undersea treasure hunters have been explorers to another world, and now they have returned to tell their tales and to display the artifacts of their adventures. We can marvel at them as we might if they had returned from a trip to Mars on an inter-planetary spaceship. For in truth, even now in 2014, we know more about the surface of Mars than we do about the vast ter-ritories of our deep Earthly oceans. And within the oceans of our blue-water planet lies all of human history waiting to be brought to the surface and made to yield us its touchstone narratives.

The primal quest of our species is to know ourselves. Astro-nauts and aquanauts are thus alike in their service to this intuitive goal. That salvors search for 17th-century Spanish galleon trea-sure in the Florida Keys is a demonstration of the indomitable human spirit to explore and to solve mysteries. Undersea trea-sure hunting, however, is not for amateurs. The skills required for ultimate success are physical, technical, and intellectual and involve sailors, divers, scientists, archaeologists, and historians in a determined long-term effort of collaboration. But before a team of experts and explorers can be assembled, there must be a vision passionately articulated by uniquely driven personalities, risk takers extraordinaire, who point the way to goals beyond most human imaginations.

Adventure seekers have a different genome than most of their fellow human beings. They are programmed "to go where no one has gone before," as Gene Roddenberry recognized in his *Star Trek* explorers. Human history celebrates the great risk takers among us who demonstrate an irrepressible drive to explore and to discover the limits of our endurance and our imaginations. Each one is a determined treasure hunter although the goals may be as diverse as a scientific breakthrough, a new direction in clas-sical music, art, or literature, or even the gymnastic miracle of a quadruple spinning jump. There are those among us who dare the impossible and achieve amazing results.

Kim and Lee Fisher are a married couple who are made of such right stuff as any explorer or adventurer who came before them. The treasures that they risk their lives to find are hidden deep in the waters of New World history. The Fisher treasures unlock the history of empires and feed the basic instincts of seafarers who believe that gold awaits their most ardent seeking. Many are called to hunt treasure, but very few achieve the spectacular successes of the Fisher family.

The biographies of explorers and adventurers are very instructive in expanding our personal worldviews of the human condition and its potential for significance. Most heroic biographies, however, are written posthumously by authors who were never on the decks of discovery or in the personal company of their subjects. Much is lost in the distance of time when composing any biography, so I appreciate the rare privilege of documenting the dramatic lives of Kim and Lee Fisher while they are still in the prime years of their discoveries.

Here then is the continuing biography of a legendary treasure salvage company and the people who are leading it today into the depths of greater discovery. I promise that there are treasures to be found and that some of them may be yours.

Monty Joynes
March, 2015

First Adventure Together

Lee and Kim enjoy a crew meal in their cabin cruise off the coast of Ecuador

DURING LEE WIEGAND'S LATTER treasure-diving years in Ecuador, she had a long-distance mentor who shared his expertise with her. The initial contact had been facilitated in Pennsylvania by Lee's mother May, who had a friend named Nadine whose sister was involved in treasure diving down in Key West, Florida. The friend provided the phone number for her sister, and Lee thus met Dolores Fisher. Dolores introduced Lee to her husband Mel, and in their first telephone conversation of some 45 minutes, Lee encountered a very generous sharer of treasure diving knowledge. Then Mel suggested that Lee talk to Fay Field, who briefed her on the uses of his magnetometer for more than an hour. All this attention, and the subsequent years of advice, was not on the clock, and no compensation was ever asked. One could easily suspect that the law of synchronicity was at work in these encounters considering that Dolores and Mel Fisher would one day become Lee's in-laws.

In June of 1985, the Fisher family was front-page news all over the world. They had found the Mother Lode after 16 years of searching for the 1622 wreckage of the Spanish treasure galleon, the *Nuestra Señora de Atocha*. For Lee, the news had a wow-factor of ten! The finders of the richest treasure of all time were people whom she knew and had talked to for several years. The Fishers' hard-earned success as the result of patient and persistent efforts encouraged Lee to organize her 9th expedition to Ecuador. For this attempt in 1986, Lee wanted support from Mel Fisher's organization as the undisputed leader in the treasure salvage industry. With investment backing, Lee leased a magnetometer that could be towed behind a boat on a cable. The equipment would be air freighted to the seacoast city of Guayaquil, where it would be serviced and operated by an experienced member of the Mel Fisher team—his own son Kim.

The beginning of their first expedition together was not auspicious. Just getting their dive and search equipment through Ecuadorian customs was an ordeal. Then Kim discovered that the carefully crated magnetometer had been damaged in transit. When tested, it would not function. At their hotel, one with no air-conditioning, the heat was oppressive, and the mosquitoes were worse. There were mosquito nets over the beds, but they were full of holes. The days of frustration with customs agents were made more tormenting by the nightly battle with the biting mosquitoes.

The second hotel was air-conditioned and offered a hot shower. The shower hot water heater was mounted above the showerhead, with an open contact lever within reach. Wet and ungrounded, a person could get the electric shock of his life when he engaged the switch. Welcome to Ecuador!

It took a full week to hire support boats and native helpers and to provision the expedition for its first week on the

Lee relaxes between treasure dives in Ecuador

island. Instead of camping out, Kim and Lee hired an old yacht to provide a kitchen and sleeping quarters. A rented Boston whaler would serve as their workboat. Since the magnetometer was damaged, their primary search device was a large loop pulse detector that could be dragged along the sand bottom on a sled. The beach extended into the water on a slope that went to 200 ft. Beyond was the edge of the continental shelf and a sudden drop-off to thousands of feet of depth that was confirmed by the passing of a pod of painted whales.

The laborious search technique was to take the loop sled out to the deep end of the slope by the Boston whaler, drop it with its attached buoy, and then haul it hand-over-hand over the search course by rope from the shore. Wherever the pulse device indicated a hit, the whaler would drop a buoy to mark the spot so that the divers could then explore it. By the end of the first week, the search routine was established and hopes were high.

On their first re-supply run to Manta, Lee and Kim heard reports that a rebellion was brewing. It was not unusual by the standards of Ecuador's coup-studded history, so they decided to return to the island and continue operations. A mail boat then stopped on the island, and a uniformed woman approached the dive team and asked Lee and Kim for their dive permits. They professed no knowledge of permits, and the woman departed. Kim assessed that a country in turmoil would not be overly concerned with permits, so they didn't worry about it.

Back on the mainland, a serious coup with potential for a violent civil war was developing. General Frank Vargas, popular Military Chief of Staff and head of the Ecuadorian Air Force, confronted the defense minister and the army commander and demanded their resignations for the abuse of public funds. Vargas was then fired for insubordination. His response was to buzz the capitol building in Quito with three

Israeli-built Kfir jets, thus sparking fears of an armed rebellion. A cat-and-mouse game then occurred as Vargas evaded two deadlines to surrender to the Ecuadorian president. His trail led to Manta where there was an air base. Manta was Kim and Lee's supply-base town, so if Manta became a battleground, they would certainly find themselves in harm's way.

When the couple returned to Manta for a second supply run, there were armed soldiers in the streets, and they were told that the army was preparing to attack the nearby air force base at Manta. The decision was made to leave the equipment in trust to their native workers for later shipment to Miami, and to get the first flight out of Guayaquil. They had only two flight options, so they went for the one going to Costa Rica. The quick escape had left them salt encrusted and poorly dressed, but they felt safe once in the air. There was no happy landing, however. On touchdown, the front-wheel landing gear malfunctioned, and the plane shuddered violently as the tire disintegrated. The aircraft stopped, and the shakened passengers had to depart the damaged plane while still on the runway. Kim remembers getting to an air-conditioned hotel in Costa Rica and spending an hour in the shower to wash away the layers of salt sweat and the accumulation of stress.

When the dive tanks finally arrived back in Miami, U.S. Customs agents opened each tank and inspected it for drugs. Ecuador was always a place of suspicion, both in the coming and in the going. In the months that followed, Lee heard unusual sounds whenever she made a personal telephone call. She suspected that her calls were being monitored. Such may be the reward for frequent foreign travel.

Who Owns Abandoned Shipwrecks?

DIVING ON SHIPWRECKS TO recover valuable property has existed since merchant vessels began to sail on ancient trade routes. The first salvors practiced breath holding and were only able to work relatively shallow depths. The invention of scuba gear in the modern era then altered the legal and moral aspects of shipwreck salvage, especially if the goal was treasure hunting. Even admiralty law that had stood the test of hundreds of years was challenged by governments eager to claim rights to shipwrecks they had previously ignored and were totally incapable of salvaging themselves. Legislative power mixed with greed demonstrated an insatiable desire for possession. The battle for rights to the extremely valuable shipwreck artifacts of the *Atocha* that were recovered in United States waters was ultimately decided by the U.S. Supreme Court. That landmark Fisher family case, however, did not settle the worldwide debate nor the legal actions that address the ultimate question: who owns abandoned shipwrecks?

Generally, a lost or sunken ship becomes "abandoned" when sufficient time has passed during which the owners have demonstrated no intention of recovery. In recent history, a vessel cannot be considered abandoned as long as an insurance company is investigating the cause of its sinking and the possibility of a total salvage. The exception for U.S. military vessels is that they are never abandoned simply through the passage of time. They must be officially stricken from the Navy list. Otherwise, wherever the vessel lies, it is protected from any encroachment. The same immunity is also granted to foreign warships, even enemy vessels, lost in U.S. waters. Today, the government of Spain claims rights over any vessel of any era that is carried on its official list of warships.

There is a 1998 case involving two Spanish wrecks off the Virginia coast that were being salvaged by Sea Hunt, Inc. The first shipwreck was the *La Galga* that ran ashore on Assateague Island September 5, 1750. Legend credits horses from the *La Galga* as the original stock from which wild horses still roam on Assateague. Their presence was made famous by the book *Misty of Chincoteague*, published in 1947, and by the feature film of the same name released in 1961. The second vessel in question was the *Juno*, a 34-gun frigate of the Spanish Navy that sank 250 miles off the Outer Banks island on October 28, 1802.

The U.S. Federal Court in the Southern District of Virginia ruled in the Sea Hunt case that there was no proof of finding and no foundation for the granting of Virginia permits to explore a six square-mile area adjoining Assateague. Sea Hunt had identified no specific wrecks. The threshold issue was "what ship?" And so in a seeming contradiction of admiralty law, the U.S. court denied its own citizens in favor of the Spanish government. "If the artifacts brought to the court came from a Spanish ship, they belonged to Spain," the court said in July 2000 as it awarded both the *La Galga* and the *Juno* to the foreign claimants.

In another significant case, beginning in 2007, an American salvage company again went up against the Spanish government and all its diplomatic and military resources. The shipwreck vessel involved was Spain's naval warship *Nuestra Señora de las Mercedes*, lost in combat in 1804 while in transit to Cadiz, Spain from Peru. The *Mercedes* was sunk by the British off the coast of Portugal in about 3,000 feet of water. She was carrying an estimated 17 tons of silver. Odyssey Marine Exploration, Inc., based in Tampa, Florida, found the wreck on the seabed in international waters near Cape Saint Mary, recovered artifacts estimated at $600 million, and then flew it to their headquarters in Tampa where it filed an admiralty salvage claim. Odyssey, the court held, purposefully withheld the crucial identity of the vessel and defiantly resisted all the court's mandates to find facts in the case. In effect, Odyssey was gambling that possession of the treasure would at the very least lead to a compromise sharing of the $600 million. Spain, however, was rumored to be pressuring the U.S. State Department and even the President, saying that good relations, and even the lease on the American base at Rota, were in jeopardy if her claims to the *Mercedes* were not honored. In a September 2013 court order, Odyssey not only lost the treasure artifacts, but it also was ordered to pay Spain's attorney fees, expenses, and costs associated with their efforts since 2007. The staggering loss to Odyssey was a warning to all treasure salvors to know the international shipwreck rules and to abide by them.

Another obstacle to shipwreck treasure salvage has been the October 2001 United Nations Educational, Scientific, and Cultural Organization (UNESCO) Convention that affords protection to shipwrecks older than 100 years. UNESCO estimates that about three million wrecks lie on the world's seabeds and that attitudes and practices regarding these vessels are out of step with land archaeology. As of an October 2011 survey, the nations who have ratified the UNESCO Convention represent only about five percent of the world's coastline. Most historic interest is in ships from the 15th, 16th, and 17th centuries, but no consideration is offered on who will pay for the salvage of these ancient ships. No government to date has volunteered to underwrite what is obviously a costly and risky business.

The concerns for shipwreck vessels as sacred burial grounds belies the fact that there are no human remains after a hundred years or more in the sacrificial elements of the sea. Corrosive chemicals, marine organisms, sand, sweeping currents, and destructive storms reduce flesh and bone back to their base elements. Deterioration will ultimately claim all evidence of human maritime heritage unless it is conserved and removed to a controlled environment.

Academic underwater archaeologists claim that they are public servants and work in a democratic system of peer review with ethical practices. From their point of view, shipwrecks should be treated as living museums in the sea, and whenever possible, should be left where they came to rest . . . so that academic archaeologists can make careers, obtain grants, and be promoted in the very competitive field of their profession. Don't they also have reputation and income incentives with regard to shipwrecks? If salvors practice high archaeological standards in their shipwreck recoveries, why should academic professionals supersede them in controlling the wreck site? Shipwreck looting and grave robbing are to be condemned by everyone, but professional salvors with records of good artifact stewardship should not be numbered among them.

Academics should play their role, but they should not supersede admiralty law and dictate the terms of free enterprise.

The responsible professional salvor has this response to those in the academic and legislative world who would judge him. Here is what the Fishers say.

"Every artifact that we find on a shipwreck, from an iron spike to a gold bar, we handle with the utmost integrity. We developed many of the archaeological guidelines for salvage in the past 50 years. We have archaeologists and conservationists on staff. If we didn't recover the historic artifacts, they would still be deteriorating on the bottom of the ocean. We get no grant money or taxpayer dollars to do all the recovery, conservation, and preservation work that we do on historic shipwrecks. Most of what has been learned from shipwrecks has been made possible by salvors who took all the life and death risks at their own expense. Shipwrecks of antiquity rightly belong to those who find them, work them, and bring back their treasures in whatever form to the mainstream of human awareness. And there is no awareness without discovery."

Kim's Childhood

KIM DOES NOT REMEMBER much about his early childhood in California where his father and mother were pioneers in scuba driving at Mel's Aqua Shop. Mel designed, built, and sold CO_2 powered spear guns, sold diving equipment, filled dive tanks, and organized the Sharks Underwater Adventure Club to dive on wrecks off the California coast. As a well-known spear fisherman, Mel hosted his own weekly television show and did the under-water photography himself. By the mid-1950s scuba opened up a new and exciting avenue for undersea exploration. The business at his Redondo Beach shop prompted Mel to create a scuba-training course and *Blue Continent*, an instructional film. As many as 65,000 people were certified by the first public diving school in the United States. And, of course, Mel's Aqua Shop sold them everything that they needed to go exploring underwater.

One very successful promotion of their entrepreneurship was Deo Fisher's record-setting endurance dive in the Hermosa Beach Aquarium tank. Deo stayed underwater in scuba gear for

55 hours and 37 minutes. She was only 23 years old at the time, and her great beauty and true grit attracted a lot of media attention. Deo was also pregnant at the time. Soon young women all over California were getting into scuba gear.

Mel always needed new stories and film for his Los Angeles television show *High Road to Danger* so there were expedition dive trips to Puerto Rico, the Virgin Islands, and Panama to cite a few. By the time Mel met Kip Wagner and had learned about the Spanish galleon treasure being recovered off the east coast of Florida, Mel was already primed to be a full-time treasure hunter. Within 90 days of making their decision, Mel and Deo sold their dive shop, mail-order business, salvage boat, and all their store merchandise. The six-car caravan, whose passengers and drivers included crewmembers from their previous expeditions, set off for the nine-day road trip to Florida.

The driver of the Fishers' Cadillac was Demosthenes Molinar, who was called Mo by the Fisher crew. Mo was a stocky black Spanish-speaking Panamanian, a diesel engine mechanic by trade, who had signed on for treasure hunting after repairing an engine on Mel's California boat, *The Golden Doubloon*. Mo was so cheerful, skillful, and industrious that Mel took him into the Caribbean and beyond as a permanent member of the Fisher team. Mo became a certified diver and later participated in every major treasure find, including the *Atocha* Mother Lode.

Kim, even at age 7, was shocked when the dark-skinned Mo was refused service in Louisiana and Alabama at both restaurants and motels. He remembers that a sympathetic restaurant cook brought a meal out to Mo in the car. It was the first time in his life that Kim had witnessed racial prejudice; and if he remembers little else about the move to Florida, he remembers his friend Mo being ostracized as they crossed the Southern states in 1963.

Poetic Vulnerability

ALL THE PEOPLE WHOM we know have exterior lives and interior lives. We relate to their appearance and their behavior, and we form opinions about them. Their interior lives, however, are revealed only in rare moments of vulnerability and creativity. Lee Fisher revealed her inmost self in a series of 58 poems written as a teenager through her late twenties. All of the poems were written with someone special in mind.

"The idea is to secure a sense of being understood," she wrote. "When things seem so unsure, it is always nice to know someone, somewhere, has been through it also; you're not alone."

As the middle child with four siblings, there was perpetual change in the family of a Navy officer on active duty during the WWII to Vietnam War years. Lee felt that her childhood required her to constantly adapt to new circumstances just to survive as an individual. She remembers the move from the southern comfort of Little Rock Air Force Base in Arkansas to Long Island, New York as the culture shock of her life. Lost was the natural environment of woods and lakes as a playground. It was replaced by concrete streets where being cool and tough was required for social survival. The formal social and religious manners that Lee had learned from a British mother and a Naval officer father did not equip her to deal with a radically new and challenging environment. Every day Lee experienced personal risks and difficult emotional choices.

When schoolmates would drop their pretenses and admit that they were also struggling, Lee sought a way to express their mutual feelings. Her method was the writing of poems, and once she had begun, she continued writing episodically for more than ten years. Then some thirty years later, she rediscovered the poems and found in them messages to herself as well as to those she had originally attempted to comfort and honor. The collected poems were published in 2006 under the name J Lee. The small book was titled *Just a Thought*. The acknowledgment page reads, "To everyone who has ever shared an encouraging word—I give many thanks, for it is the frequency of Love, which energizes this work."

Teenage friend Andi and Lee decide to hitchhike to Florida

The meter of the poems is usually iambic with alternating rhyming lines. The form may be simple, but the emotional intensity is complex. Among the six poems relating to her parents, the poem "To Mom . . . Going "My Way" is illustrative of how Lee gets to the heart of a young adult's struggle for identity. This poem came about when Lee announced her intention to hitchhike from their home in Pennsylvania to Key West.

"Why don't you just take your car?" her father asked.

"I can't explain it," Lee replied. "It's just something I have to do."

Her mother's reaction was to cry, and Lee's subsequent poem became her way to respond. Lee, in fact, did hitchhike to Key West with her best friend Andi, short for Andrea. She recalls the trip as a "magical adventure."

> *I thank you Mom for your concern,*
> *But there are lessons I must learn,*
> *And answers no one else can teach,*
> *Ones only I alone can reach.*
> *No matter what they all might say,*
> *Experience is the better way*
> *For me to find the dreams I seek,*
> *Fulfill this task and find some peace.*
> *Though it may seem I've gone astray,*
> *I hope you'll understand one day.*
> *There's one more thing I'd like to say.*
> *I Love You so in my own way.*

Some poems reflect Lee's Presbyterian church upbringing with its concepts of predestination.

TIME
Tho time on earth
May pass us by;
Eternity waits
On the other side.

REALITY
Imagination is the key
For you to create reality;
Act as if and it will be
Now and through eternity.

There are also verses in the "love poem" category, but the object of her affection is not named. Youthful romantic love always seems to be unrequited. In these poems, there is expressed a longing for a soulmate. As her life evolved, Lee would wait until her mid-thirties to find the one companion who could fulfill her poetic dreams.

Lee with her father Vic

5

Kim's Teenage Years

THE FISHER FAMILY'S FIRST full salvage season in 1964 off the Ft. Pierce Inlet was proving the worth of Fay Field's electronic magnetometer in detecting metal objects on the ocean floor. Mel and Fay also invented a prop wash deflector that they named a "mailbox" to blow clear water to the bottom and to displace sand so as to expose treasure. Their mailbox invention became the primary tool in treasure salvage. When their salvage efforts started producing cannons, silver coins, and gold disks from the 1715 Spanish fleet, the State of Florida began a policy of intervention to claim and control all treasure found in its territorial waters. It was a legal battle that would last for years, and in the case of the *Atocha*, it would go all the way to the U.S. Supreme Court.

In June of 1964, the Fisher salvors made international news. Mo, the dark-skinned Panamanian who had been refused service in the South during their trip from California to Florida, dove on a mailbox-cleared pothole in the sand to find "a carpet of gold." There were coins everywhere. Gold doubloons the size of contemporary silver dollars. 1,033 coins that day, and 900 more the next. The coins that ranged in dates between 1699 and 1715 were scattered all over the reef. They were part of the treasure of a Spanish galleon fleet that had been shipwrecked in a 1715 hurricane.

Kim was nine years old when the *National Geographic Magazine* feature story "Treasure Coast" was published in January 1965. The term "treasure coast" still stands today. The color photos of the gold coins and jewelry discovered in 1964 set off gold fever along the Florida east coast and tempted pirate divers to violate the Fisher sites. The public attention also started a treasure war. Political players in the Florida government wanted to re-write the laws regarding shipwreck salvage and claim everything for the State. *The Miami Herald* then characterized Mel Fisher's salvage group as a band of thieves who were stealing from the State. Never mind that the 1715 treasure had sat on the ocean bottom for 250 years without a single effort by the State of Florida to recover it. Never mind that the Fisher group members had risked their personal fortunes to find the treasure. Never mind that they

Photo by Mel Fisher's Treasures

Captain Kim of the Southwind

had revolutionized the underwater salvage industry by their new inventions. Never mind "finders keepers" or admiralty law.

Kim remembers the day that the carpet of gold coins was found. His baby sister Taffi had recently been celebrated for her third birthday. Mel came home that day and called his four children around him. Kim remembers a purple towel that had been rolled up. With a bit of flourish, their father unrolled the towel to reveal a long row of pure gold coins. Then he spread the coins out for them to touch and admire. His instruction to them was not to tell anyone about the gold. The treasure was to be kept a secret. Kim says that he, Dirk, Kane, and even little Taffi could not get away fast enough to tell their friends.

"We learned that week that it is impossible to keep found treasure a secret," Kim says.

That year at age nine, Kim made his first dive on a treasure site.

"I was diving in a hole dug by the mailbox. The engine was running at idle to provide a "bubble" of clear water. Mo Molinar took me to a spot in the hole where the sand that was washing out was black. I had been told earlier that oxidizing silver coins turned the sand around them black. I started hand-fanning the pocket of black sand, and sure enough, a silver coin appeared. It was an incredible moment that I will always

remember. The thrill of being the first person to see that coin in 250 years. I had found my first treasure, and I immediately was addicted to that feeling. I wanted to find more. I still have that same desire today, to bring that history to the surface and share it with other people."

Finding a silver coin is one thing. Finding gold is even better. As Kim remembers, it takes your breath away.

"I remember the excitement of my first dives, and then I found a piece of gold. I was hooked on treasure hunting from that day forward. Even today, the thrill level remains the same. Once, when I was free diving, I started picking treasure coins out of the mud and couldn't stop. I held my breath so long that it frightened my dad. When I popped to the surface, he gave me a very heated lecture. It was one of the few times that I ever saw him get upset or angry."

By the end of 1965, the partnership of Mel's Treasure Salvors and Kip Wagner's Real Eight had salvaged among other riches over 37,000 individual silver coins, a 250-pound chest of silver coins, 1782 gold coins, 41 copper disks, and 29 silver wedges. But there would be no cash from sales for many months until a division with the State of Florida was made. By contract, the State was entitled to 25% of a division—the first division of treasure in a state that had never done it before.

There are many treasure *seekers* but few treasure *finders*. But when you do find treasure, your troubles really begin. You can deal with prolonged disappointments and the threats of bankruptcy, but how do you defend yourself against the onslaught of egos, greed, and bureaucracy?

When the 1715 wreck sites stopped producing, and the Florida government imposed bonds on salvors, daily logs, artifact tagging, and state agents assigned to each salvage boat that worked within the three-mile state jurisdiction, Mel Fisher looked to the outer reefs of the Keys that came under less restrictive Federal laws. For Mel, the Keys beckoned with its warm, clear waters all year and its shipwrecks scattered all over the charts. The year was 1968, and Mel decided to go for the big prize—The *Atocha*.

"Mel never gave up on the 1715 fleet wrecks. He eventually ended up buying out Real Eight's interest in those wrecks. Taffi and I sold those wreck sites just a few years ago. He kept working them during the summer season. There are only about 100 days a year when the weather is good enough to make working the 1715 fleet wrecks economically feasible. The rest of the year it is just not cost effective to keep a boat and crew on standby to work the very few days that it is calm enough.

"During the winter when it was too rough to work the 1715 fleet wrecks, he would go down to the Florida Keys and search for the *Atocha*.

"The whole family actually went to the Keys during the winter. The first year we rented a house in Marathon, and we all went to school there for part of the year and in Vero Beach for part of the year. The next winter we went to Islamorada, again spending part of the school year at each location. The third winter it was Tavernier. After that, Gene Lyon found the research that moved the operation to Key West."

Mel and Deo attended a Bible study class at the newly organized Methodist church in Vero Beach. The teacher was Eugene Lyon. As a graduate student of Spanish colonial history, Gene had learned to read the archaic script of the 17th century. Mel owned old Spanish books about shipwrecks that he could not decipher. Gene could read them. The synchronicity of their mutual interests led to a huge breakthrough in 1970. Working on his doctorate at the Archives of the Indies in Seville, Spain, Gene discovered documents that put the *Atocha* and its 1622 shipwrecked companion galleon, the *Santa Margarita*, forty miles west of Key West in the vicinity of the Marquesas Key. The search for the *Atocha* shifted 100 miles to the west, and the Fisher family would spend the next fifteen years exploring around the Marquesas out of sight of land before they hit the Mother Lode.

Imagine, if you can, that you are a 16-year-old Vero Beach high school student in 1972. When summer comes, you and your older 19-year-old brother Dirk room together on a smaller houseboat moored to your parents' houseboat in Key West. You are a certified scuba diver and an accomplished boat captain. Since your earliest childhood memories, you have participated in your father's passion for treasure hunting. You and your entire family have a short calm-water season to search for two of the richest Spanish treasure galleons in New World history. The *Nuestra Señora de Atocha* and the *Santa Margarita* sank off the Florida Keys in 1622. Your father calls you to work everyday with the phrase, "Today's the day!" You heed the call because you have already dived for treasure and found it.

This year you are sent to New Orleans with crews to bring back two Mississippi River tugboats with big, powerful engines. Your father's invention called "mailboxes" would be lowered over the big props of the tug and dig holes in the bottom sand to expose the treasure. The two tugs, the 59-ft. *Southwind*, and the 54-ft. *Northwind*, however, were never designed to work in open ocean. They were too low in the water with a tall pilothouse that would roll violently in high waves.

Kim recalls his adventure with the two tugboats in a very concise style that invites us to imagine the drama of it between the lines.

"Actually Dirk was not on that trip. It was Chet Alexander, Rick Vaughn and myself. We went up to New Orleans and spent eight days getting the boats ready for the trip. When we left the Mississippi River and entered the Gulf of Mexico, it was actually pretty calm. We were using the *Northwind* to tow the *Southwind* because we only had three guys. We ran four-hour shifts, the first shift at the helm, the second shift in the engine room, and the third shift sleeping. Then we repeated it 24 hours a day.

"In the middle of the first night, one of the engines on the *Northwind* cut out, and the boat circled around and got the tow rope in the prop. Cutting the rope out was quite exciting in the middle of the night in a thousand feet of water without scuba gear. We had a small compressor for a paint sprayer, and I had to hold it just above the surface of the water so that Chet could reach the propeller. He simply stuck the end of the hose in his mouth and used it to supply air to him while he sawed the rope out of the prop. After cutting the rope, Chet decided that we should transfer to the *Southwind* and use it to tow the *Northwind*.

"The seas picked up a little, and since the boats had never been out of the rivers, the sludge in the bottom of the fuel tanks got churned up and kept clogging up the fuel filters. We kept changing the filters until we ran out and then had to call the coast guard to tow us into Pensacola. We spent two days there cleaning the fuel tanks and getting more filters. We decided to follow the coast instead of going straight from Pensacola to Key West. After that, it was a smooth trip following the coast down to Fort Myers and then cutting across Florida Bay to Key West."

Now imagine yourself as Kim. You turn seventeen, and you are named captain of the *Southwind*. Your 19-year-old brother becomes captain of the *Northwind,* and Kane, your 13-year-old brother, becomes a member of your crew. You are doing the work of a man with leadership responsibilities among men and women in what is considered a dangerous occupation: salvage at sea.

What is a great sea story without romance? Kim, described as quiet and serious, was still available to romance. And what a catch for any girl. He was tall, tanned, and good-looking, plus he was the captain of a big boat bringing in Spanish galleon treasure. His older brother Dirk had the same credentials. They were both living an enviable lifestyle, an over-the-moon lifestyle that any teenager would love to experience.

A Michigan college man working with the Fishers recommended that a family friend join the summer seasonal treasure hunting crew. Jo Arden Stuart came to cook aboard the *Southwind*, but she was also a skilled artist who could accurately sketch the artifacts that the divers recovered. The *Northwind* female crewmember was Angel Curry, also shipping on as a cook. Angel was skilled at organizing, so she also kept the detailed ship's log and dive records. It is fair to say from photographs of that time that both women were close to gorgeous—one blonde to match Dirk's long blonde hair, and the other a brunette like Kim.

The routine on the *Southwind* was to stay on the *Atocha* dive sites for weeks at a time. Essentials came by supply boat, and the big boat didn't return to Key West except to refuel and recondition. The at-sea workdays were long and hard, but at the end of their labors were a good hot meal and a few beers to wash away the muscle aches. The interaction between the team members was necessarily intimate due to the close quarters for sleeping and bathing. The garments of choice during those hot-weather days at sea were bathing suits for both men and women. Nothing, as they say, was left to the imagination. Nudity was one garment slip away. Is it any wonder the beautiful young people fall in love in those circumstances? And so it happened. Dirk fell in love with Angel, and Kim fell in love with Jo. The treasure season that year with all its triumphs must have seemed magical to the young lovers. They were living the best teenage romantic movie ever made!

In July Dirk and Angel married on board the *Golden Doubloon* docked at a marina in Old Town Key West. The large wooden ship had been purchased in Sweden and rebuilt topside to resemble a Spanish galleon. The ship with its displays of treasure artifacts served as a tourist attraction, retail jewelry outlet, and executive offices. The evening sunset wedding was conducted on the quarterdeck of the galleon. Kim was his brother's best man, and Jo was one of Angel's bridesmaids. Over one hundred guests attended, and Mel and Deo Fisher were pleased for their eldest son. Angel happily joined the crew of her 20-year-old husband's salvage tug, the *Northwind*.

Then in April 1974, Kim at 18 married Jo at her hometown in Michigan. Following their honeymoon, Kim was anxious to get back to the *Southwind*. Treasure hunting was in his blood, and he did not want to miss a day of the salvage season when the wind and weather made open-water treasure hunting possible. Marriage, with babies on the horizon, however, was a compromise to Kim's freewheeling days as one of Key West's most visible treasure hunters.

Then, too, treasure hunting, even as a boat captain and a Fisher family member, was not always a stable occupation as his own father had proved. How many times over the years had his father faced bankruptcy, and his family and crews lived close to the poverty line? Jo had come for a summer of risky adventure. Was she now prepared for a lifetime of it?

6

The Key West State of Mind

KEY WEST IS TODAY a state of mind as much as it is a tropical tourist playground. At Mallory Square facing the waters of the Gulf of Mexico where there is a nightly gala to celebrate the sunset, 16th-century Spanish fishermen from colonial Cuba once camped during their excursions for fish, manatees, and the tasty meat and eggs of sea turtles and birds. Rich, bustling Havana was the major market for their goods. But even before the Spanish, there were the Indians who fished and farmed on the southernmost point of the Keys. The Indians, who could be considered the original Key West pirates, were feared as they preyed on the small boats from Cuba and prospered from the ships that wrecked on the key's dangerous reef.

The history of America started in these Atlantic and Gulf of Mexico waters. From the discoveries of Christopher Columbus in 1492 that included Cuba, to Ponce de Leon's expedition to the Florida Keys in 1513, Western cultural awareness of North and South America begins here. The English settlement at Jamestown on the York River in Virginia, for example, dates from 1607. By that date, St. Augustine on the Florida east coast and Havana, Cuba were important Spanish colonial ports.

Key West as a city was not founded until 1822, but it had existed as Cayo Hueso, the Isle of Bones. The Spanish had named it because of the skeletal remains uncovered in a vast Indian graveyard. By the mid-1800s, New Englanders and Bahamians had rushed to Key West to cash in on the salvaging of millions of dollars of cargoes from shipwrecks on the reefs. These salvors were called "wreckers" and they made Key West one of the richest cities in America during their heyday. Wrecker success by 1860 gave rise to a substantial cigar industry. At one time there were 165 cigar factories primarily operated by Cuban immigrants.

Key West, although booming in the shipwreck and salvage business, was not yet a popular destination. The town, built on coral reef, limestone, and mangrove swamps was then swarming with mosquitoes, and the residential architecture might be termed driftwood-shipwreck happenstance. Henry Flagler, the great Florida visionary, however, had his mind and money set on extending his Florida East Coast Railway south from Miami to the underdeveloped deep-water port at Key West. It took seven years, but in 1912 the first steam train crossed key after key along the 153-mile route to Key West. Now the door was open, and a general vacationing public was able to reach its tropical environs.

Although a hurricane packing 200-mile-per-hour winds pushed an 18-foot tidal wave across the upper Keys and destroyed the railroad, its right-of-way would be used to construct an overseas highway that was completed a few years before the entry of the United States into WWII. Key West was an important military base, and many Navy families became residents of Key West. Note the "Fly Navy" building on Trumbo Point. The post-war years after 1945 began a period of rapid development of Key West as a tourist destination. Restaurants and resort hotels flourished, and elegant yachts and world-class charter fishing boats were seen in all the developing marinas. In 2014, the Key West Chamber of Commerce expected one million tourists to visit who would be served by a Key West resident population of 25,000.

But don't let the polished glitter of resort attractions distract you. The native Saltwater Conchs and the long-term resident Freshwater Conchs believe that they are members of the Conch Republic, and they have their own flag and passports to attest to a time when they felt that the Federal government was not protecting them from a modern invasion of refugees from Cuba during the Mariel Boatlift of 1980. But the Conch Republic is less political than it is a place and a state of mind. It is a place in that it is where they live and work and raise a family. It is a state of mind because they feel independent from the proprieties of the mainland and even rebellious against its conformity. There is always *mañana*, which means "not today" in their minds. There is always another day in the palm and banyan tree end-of-the-world, island-like paradise.

"Do not rush me," a Conch might say. "I have friends to see, and stories to tell. Yes, I will linger over a Mojito or a Cuba Libre or two at a hidden tiki bar beside a marina. I will find out about the fishing, and I will smoke a really good cigar regardless of the expense. Hey, anyway, it's not too pricey to drink and smoke when you get the Conch discount. We take care of each other, bubba.

"And if I make myself look like a zombie with gruesome makeup and tattered clothes and slide down Duval Street with five or six thousand other Conchs and our friends, what's the purpose other than to laugh? Be alive. Express yourself. Why else would you want to live in Key West?

"We work hard and then we party harder. Maybe it has something to do with the dangers of working on a shrimp boat or a charter boat out in the Gulf Stream trolling for sailfish or tuna. The storms in these waters are unpredictable. And then there are the annual hurricanes that threaten us. What are you going to do? We've got salt water in our veins. We're pirates and shipwreck salvagers to our core. We don't deny it. We celebrate it. And as a Conch, somewhere deep inside we recognize that we are all in these circumstances together, so why not live and let live? Let go of your judgments. Lighten up. Join the fun.

"Slow down. It's an island. You are just going in circles anyway. No one cares what you look like but you. And if you are wearing a tie, you are either a first-time visitor or you are going to court. Ok, we know that a Key is not an island, but we'll call it an island for your sake. And if you ask for directions, we'll refer you north and south when we know that you are actually traveling east and west. Trust us because we are glad that you are here."

Doctor Juanita Lee Wiegand

JUANITA LEE WIEGAND WAS ALREADY a certified scuba diver
when she graduated from nursing school as a Licensed Graduate
Practical Nurse (LGPN) at age 20 in 1975. Nursing was a good
occupation for a young adventurous woman because its knowledge and skill sets could be transferred to any part of the country.
Nursing was also a flexible job with regard to scheduling. When
adventure called, Juanita Lee could take a hiatus from her hospital
and be sure that a nursing position would open up on her return.

The problem about being a LGPN in a busy hospital is that
you may be viewed at the bottom of the professional medicine
totem pole by Registered Nurses (RNs) and especially by doctors. The judgments and opinions of a smart, vibrant and independent young woman like Juanita Lee are neither wanted nor
welcomed in the hierarchy of a hospital. At times Juanita Lee
felt that she was invisible as she worked side-by-side with senior
nurses and doctors. There was no doubt that her contributions

to patient care were being marginalized in a health care system that even the United States Congress had termed "broken."

Like most challenges in her life, Juanita Lee believed that she could take medicine head-on, but as a hospital staff LGPN, she realized that she had no authority to serve patients in an enlightened way. She was stuck in a male-dominated work environment where her ideas and initiatives were both ignored and chastised. The desire then rose up in her to take control of her career and move in a direction where she, herself, could make decisions about patient care.

Juanita Lee became interested in chiropractic medicine when her brother Rick attended the Palmer College of Chiro-

Photo by Art Gentile, Montgomery Newspapers

practic in Davenport, Iowa. Rick's enthusiasm propelled her to investigate a profession that most doctors in the early 1980s considered unscientific. Whenever she mentioned her new interest to hospital associates, they immediately expressed skepticism. Most MDs did not have knowledge nor an understanding of what chiropractors did for their patients, and yet they stood

Doctors Robert and Juanita Wiegand

against it. It was not until 1980 that the American Medical Association reluctantly allowed its members to refer patients to chiropractors. Up until that time, the antagonism between chiropractic and the traditional medical profession facilitated a line that could not be crossed. Now, Juanita Lee intended to cross that line and attempt to join an even more eccentric group—female chiropractors.

While taking courses at the Adio Institute of Chiropractic in Langhorne, Pennsylvania, Juanita Lee maintained her hospital job as a means of support. Her work schedule was hard, and the chiropractic courses in anatomy and other subjects were the same as those taken by medical students. Both the academic and the practical aspects of earning a chiropractic degree were challenging. There was a two-year period when her financial resources were so stretched that she had no heat in her apartment and subsisted with the aid of food stamps. That poverty experience was later to give her profound insights into the lives of the struggling poor.

Juanita Lee graduated in 1982 from chiropractic college and joined her brother Rick in establishing a joint practice in a farmhouse that they renovated in three months. The Doctors Wiegand—he 31 and she 28—now operated The Huntingdon Valley Chiropractic Center that opened for patient care in February 1983. Finally, Nurse Juanita Lee had become Doctor Juanita Lee, and her future as an independent woman was assured. Her destiny as an adventurer and explorer, however, was to take her across the world, and her chiropractic practice well served her as an income platform to launch those adventures.

A Formal Education Detour

AFTER ALL THE PROMISING treasure finds of the early 1970s on a trail that the Fishers believed would lead them to the *Atocha* Mother Lode, the salvage company hit financial rock-bottom in mid-August 1974, as their treasure wealth was tied up in court adjudication. Then came the dramatic discovery of the *Atocha* bronze cannons by Kim's brother Dirk on the 18th of July 1975. The proof that the *Atocha* had been found made headlines around the world, and the Fisher family's triumph over the Spanish treasure galleon was both justified and ecstatically joyful. Two days later, with Dirk and his wife Angel back over the *Atocha* cannon site on the *Northwind*, the greatest tragedy of the Fisher family occurred when the salvage tug capsized before dawn and trapped Dirk, Angel, and another diver, Rick Gage, below decks.

Suddenly the Fisher clan went from the highest high to the lowest low of emotions. The distraught father, Mel, sold the *Northwind* for salvage and the *Southwind*, too, because that tug was linked too closely to the other. All treasure operations came to a halt. Many observers believed that the broken hearts would break the business, too. Everyone associated with the Fisher family had to re-evaluate their roles and their intentions to continue.

The pressure on Kim Fisher, now a captain without a boat, was to seek a more safe and secure occupation. The fork in the road of destiny presented itself, and Kim chose life with Jo in moving to her home territory to attend Central Michigan University. In the retrospective long view, Kim avoids the memory of tragic circumstances when asked today about his decision to leave Key West.

"I wanted to see what winter was like," he says with dry humor. "Three Michigan winters was enough."

Kim earned a degree in business administration with a finance major in three and a half years. He graduated in the top ten percent of his class. Being a married student with children was, however, financially difficult, but he accomplished his education goal.

The run for the sun took the Kim Fisher family to Tallahassee and the Florida State University of Law. In his two years there, Kim took the Admiralty Law, Federal and Civil Procedure, and Evidence courses that would serve him so well in later years as he defended the Fisher family salvage rights in state and Federal Courts. Kim admits that the prospect of becoming a practicing attorney did not appeal to him. He saw attorneys at work, and he didn't want to be one of them. Then a crisis intervened to alter the future direction of his life.

In 1982, Kim's father Mel went into surgery for the removal of polyps in his bladder. The polyps were malignant. The oncologist diagnosed the cancer and gave Mel Fisher perhaps less than a year to live. Kim says that he "panicked" when he got the news. He then abandoned law school to immediately return to Key West. Money was scarce as Kim returned to the treasure salvage business.

"Jo," he said, "wanted stability. I wanted to treasure hunt."

In 1983 the couple separated and then divorced. Jo took their three sons back to her home in Michigan. She later remarried.

"It was hard, and I was brokenhearted," Kim says, "but I had to follow my dreams and be loyal to my father."

The cancer death sentence that had been handed out to Mel Fisher was for him just another one of the many inconveniences that he had overcome with his indomitable optimism. Mel lived another 16 years and saw his life's ambition of finding the *Atocha* Mother Lode realized.

9

A Liberated Woman

LEE WIEGAND WORKED AS a nurse for almost a decade. Starting on the med surg floor she progressed to labor and delivery, then finished her final four years in the intensive coronary care unit. Her hospital experience, however, convinced her that she wanted to be self-employed; and so while still working as a nurse, she returned for six more years of college to become a licensed chiropractor. Family and friends who knew Lee as a determined independent woman were not surprised that she wanted liberation from a traditional 40-hour in-house work schedule.

The leap into private practice as a licensed chiropractor was a successful one, and Lee built up a business that was both profitable and complementary to a lifestyle that afforded travel and adventure. Over time, in spite of her success, Lee had larger ambitions. She envisioned a holistic health center where medical doctors, chiropractors, nutritionists, and other healing arts practitioners could offer a complementary approach to health.

Her concept was to buy a building and assemble the professional team that would practice there in a collaborative effort.

When Lee asked the medical doctors if they would see patients at the center, each one said yes. When she explained the "team" approach for evaluation and treatment planning would include MD, DC, OD, Acupuncture, Homeopathy, Nutrition, they were open to it. Lee was very excited to create a global approach to healing.

Lee worked with an investment counselor who had clients that he would place in her venture capital project. On that promise, Lee sold her chiropractic practice to finance her part of the venture and began working fulltime on the development of the holistic center. Her vision was large and perhaps ahead of its time in 1984. Then, suddenly, and without warning, changes in venture capital tax code caused the investment counselor to withdraw his clients from Lee's project. Shocked and confused, she found herself unemployed. Nevertheless, Lee was not the kind of person who accepts defeat.

When the shock of reality wore off, Lee created a new strategy to get back into the practice of chiropractic without the loss of a more liberating lifestyle. She decided to market herself as a Doctor On Call service (Doc's) who would be available to substitute for other doctors who wanted to go on vacation or take days off without closing their offices. Her overhead went from $14,000 in private practice to $64 a month with Doc's. Her new venture required only a pager and an answering service that could recite a script of her fees and conditions. She made a general announcement to the chiropractic community within a one-hour drive radius from her home that she was available to relieve doctors on a contractual basis. Then since Lee had privileges at the officers' swim club at the Willow Grove Naval Air Station, courtesy of her father, a Navy commander and pilot, she waited poolside for the answering service to contact her.

Lee had tapped a lucrative source of income, and she was free to travel around her intermittent work schedule. She had managed to create a huge free-space where she could explore her personal interests to surf Hawaii, ski the Alps, wind surf, sky dive, treasure hunt, model, back pack Europe, and achieve her black belt.

For years, the trim athletic doctor from Pennsylvania made chiropractic medicine take second place while she explored the world. Men were attracted to her intelligence and vitality, but none of them offered her a life that was not, in part, a surrender of her individuality. One adventure that lured her back repeatedly was treasure diving in Ecuador.

The Pacific Ocean coast between Peru and Colombia was a route traveled by Spanish treasure galleons for 300 years as they carried huge quantities of silver coins and 60 to 80-pound silver bars to a port on the Panama isthmus to be transported overland by mule train to the Caribbean, and then by ship to Havana where the annual treasure fleets sailed across the Atlantic to Spain. For the Dutch warship enemy, British privateers and outright pirates, the passage of the silver-laden Spanish ships provided tempting targets. Even if treasure galleons avoided combat and sinking on the trade route, they might fall victim to raging Pacific Ocean storms. Whatever the cause, among the more than 1,300 shipwrecks recorded between Peru and Colombia, perhaps as many as 200 were laden with treasure.

Lee was on her ninth expedition searching for the treasures of Sir Francis Drake when she hired some equipment from Mel Fisher. He sent his son Kim and another diver, Dick Claudt, with the equipment to Ecuador. Today when people ask Lee if she found her treasure in Ecuador, she answers, "Yes, my husband Kim."

The connection to the most celebrated family in Key West, in retrospect, is a synchronicity that ultimately brought Lee back to her birthplace. Lee Wiegand Fisher is one of the rare native-born Conchs of Key West. She was born in the Key West Naval Hospital and as a child lived on Sigsbee Naval Air Station. Wiegand home movies of Lee's father's tour in Key West show him piloting a helicopter and landing Santa Claus on the Naval base to the waiting crowds of military families.

Commander Victor Hugo Wiegand set high standards of character and fortitude for his five children. His childhood was spent in Kansas—far, far away from the flight deck of a U.S. Navy aircraft carrier. After high school, Vic, as he was called by his friends, enlisted in the Navy as an apprentice seaman. Through self-improvement and determination, he became a Naval aviation cadet and then a Naval aviation officer. On station in Norfolk, Virginia, homeport of the Atlantic Fleet, Vic met and married May McGiveron, his companion and family anchor for the next 60 years. The Wiegand home movies progressed to show Vic doing touch-and-go landings on aircraft carriers as part of his flight training each year.

A family story from Vic's days at sea tells about May waking up screaming Vic's name at two o'clock early one morning. There was no way for May to verify or justify her nighttime horror. Perhaps the wives of all Navy pilots experienced such fears. But when Vic came home, and May told him her nightmare, he was amazed. How did she know that something had gone wrong that put him in danger?

Yes, there had been a life-threatening incident during a nighttime landing. The tail hook skipped the cable, and he had crashed on deck. The deck crew pulled him out of the damaged aircraft, and by tradition, Vic was immediately put into another plane for another takeoff and carrier landing. Somehow beyond the measure of science, the bond between Vic and May provided a mystic communication that night.

Lee, as a Navy junior, was a witness to the stresses of being part of a military service family. From NAS Key West, to AFB Fort Worth, Texas, AFB Little Rock, Arkansas, NAS New York and NAS Willow Grove, Pennsylvania, she was constantly required to adjust and refocus on the circumstances at hand. As a teenager, she saw her father retired from the Navy in 1970 after 25 years of distinguished service. Then he set another example. He earned a master's degree and became an elementary school teacher for ten years.

Vic and May Wiegand demonstrated a strong sense of honor, integrity, and religious faith throughout their lives. Their legacy has prompted their children to also

pursue high ideals with determination and courage. In many ways, they fostered the liberated and adventurous woman that their daughter Lee would become.

There is an update to the legacy of Navy Commander Victor Hugo Wiegand. Lee showed her father's Navy Aviator's leather flight jacket to Kim, and he brought it into the office to show to Administrative Director Joe Sweeney. Joe, as a Navy Chief, had spent his early service years in the Navy Aviation community. He had even lived on an aircraft carrier for over six years. Joe immediately recognized the flight jacket as old and a classic. It was also in "wonderful" condition. Research of the patches on the jacket indicated that it was from the mid-1950s.

With permission, Joe then offered the rare jacket to the USS Intrepid Museum in New York and the Naval Aviation

Museum in Pensacola. Both museums "wanted it badly," Joe reports. Lee, however, wanted to keep the jacket in Florida so she chose the museum in Pensacola. Eventually, Lee found Vic's flight helmet, and that went to a very grateful Naval Aviation Museum as well.

It is informative to know how our personal artifacts represent us. A gold bosun's pipe found after more than 300 years on the ocean bottom still gives a high-pitched whistle as it did from the lips of the man who blew it. The display of a Navy Aviator's flight jacket and helmet makes us wonder who he was and what he experienced. Those who have served in the military may come to attention and salute him although we see only these few things to represent who he was.

10

The Missing Man

LEE WIEGAND IN THE early 80's was a Bucks County, Pennsylvania chiropractor who had a reputation for adventure travel. The highly expressive and animated perfect size-nine brunette had already hiked the major attractions of Europe and been to more exotic places when she enrolled in a scuba diving certification class at her local community college. Her open-water checkout dive, the final test for her dive card, was done in the Reading Quarry during February in Pennsylvania.

The master diver who taught and awarded the scuba certification must have been impressed by Lee because he enlisted her as part of his team to go treasure hunting in Ecuador. Lee would later become a full partner in their expedition, and then raise her own capital investments to underwrite nine trips to the South American Pacific coast.

Shipwreck treasure hunting always begins with historical research, and Lee and her associates spent two years delving into the reports of Sir Francis Drake's voyages of 1579 in the famed

Golden Hind. The event that offered the most potential reward was the dumping of a few tons of pure silver ingots off a small uninhabited island 14 miles off the coast of Ecuador. Sir Francis Drake, the British privateer, had captured a vast amount of silver from a Spanish treasure galleon, but the bounty dangerously overloaded his ship. To make sail back to England, Drake was forced to jettison 40 tons of silver ingots into the shallows with the intention he would return to retrieve it the following year. The recovery, however, never happened as the English crown failed to finance Drake's return trip to the other side of the world.

Other Americans were also in search of the Drake treasure, and one expedition of them had mined the silver bottom with a clam bucket crane and come away with bucket loads of silver ingots. Their crude shack and campsite was still on the island when Lee and her dive team first arrived. Lee, too, would have to transport all their diving gear, food, water, and camping supplies to the island and live rough while diving to locate the treasure site. Re-supply would be required each week on an anticipated three-week stay on the island.

The first week of the month-long expedition had been spent just getting from the international airport in Guayaquil and organizing local help in the small coastal town of Manta. The five-hour bone-quivering ride in the back of a pickup truck wedged between scuba tanks was the first test of a treasure hunter's endurance. On the scrub island itself, Ecuadorian fishing boats would often anchor overnight and share a campfire with the treasure hunters who posed as counter-cultural hippies as a cover for their real purposes.

The political tension in Ecuador was such that the fishermen whom Lee encountered were armed with both rifles and machetes. A great language-barrier misunderstanding led to one of the most bizarre and dangerous events in Lee's expedition life. Early one morning, with Lee and her partner out of sight, a group of fishermen were firing off their rifles into the surf. The third member of Lee's party, David, an investor who had financed their expedition, heard the shots and only saw enough to believe that Lee and friend were being murdered in the surf. David panicked and ran away to keep from being murdered, too. When David went missing from their campsite, Lee and her dive partner began to look for him. As the hours passed, they became alarmed as they searched the island.

Lee was able to enlist the armed fishermen to help in the search, and they formed a column of march. After a long unsuccessful trek in the unrelenting heat, the erstwhile guards stopped suddenly and "forced" Lee and friend to drink from their canteens. Then they were shoved to their knees into the shade of a low scrub bush. The rough treatment was first perceived as some kind of capture, but then Lee realized that the natives had recognized their dehydration and had taken steps to save them from collapse.

When David remained missing, Lee approached a European yacht captain anchored offshore and asked him to report the missing man to Ecuadorian officials on the mainland. Lee's party had been social with the vacationing people on the yacht. Resigned to the loss of their companion, Lee retreated to Zack's Shack, a primitive structure where a local named Zack had set up a concession to sell cigarettes and beer to the fishermen, vacation boaters, and campers who visited the island. Lee and her dive partner were drinking beer to drown the sorrow of their lost companion when something down the beach caught their attention. As if a mirage, the ghost of a figure approached.

The movement of the figure was halting and uncertain, but gradually it became clear. It was the missing man! Hungry and dehydrated, David had to be supported back to camp where he related the terror of the past two days. While evading the supposed killer fishermen, he had failed to find any water and had survived only by drinking his own urine.

With the missing man restored, and the misunderstanding cleared up, all seemed well, but then serious trouble appeared literally on the horizon.

When the mast of the Ecuadorian Navy warship broke the horizon and then grew to expose its huge mass, it was shocking. Why was such a large vessel on a direct approach to the tiny island? The Navy vessel was able to come so close to the quarter-mile-long island because at 14 miles from the mainland, the deep drop of the continent shelf was just offshore. Oops, Lee concluded, they must be coming to investigate the missing American. Unfortunately, the Ecuadorians who interrogated them spoke no English, and at that time Lee spoke no Spanish. As much as Lee and her companions tried through gestures to assure the elaborately uniformed Naval officer that there was no problem, a stern expression remained on his face, and he ordered them under armed guard to assemble their equipment and belongings and be taken aboard his warship. Thus, not only was Lee's expedition cut short, and their investor deprived of any chance of profit on his $40,000 investment, but her party also realized that they were in deep trouble. People of greater means had disappeared before in South America, so their uncertainty must have contained a very high fear factor.

It was long after dark by the time the warship reached a mainland dock where the three Americans were roughly shoved into a military truck. The captain of the warship spoke no English, and he seemed visibly perturbed by the incident that had inconvenienced him late into the night. When Lee and her two friends were taken to a military base, they feared that they were prisoners. Then to reinforce their fears, they were escorted by armed men into an interrogation room of stark grey walls and a single desk. Behind the desk sat a stern-faced Naval captain in his full dress-white uniform.

Thankfully, a translator was present, and Lee and her party were able to explain their presence on the island as vacationers and the missing man misunderstanding. They did not mention that they were treasure hunters. At the end of this session, the officer commanded each of them individually to talk to the American consul in Quito, the capital, who through official governmental channels asked to be reassured that the three Americans were safe.

Safe is a relative concept that does not imply freedom. Lee and friends were only free to lug their personal item duffle bags under guard to a barracks with bunk beds and a shower. En route to the barracks, they had another scare. David had a metal detector in his duffle bag as part of their dive gear. Somehow it got switched on and rang out its alert sound as it detected one of the guards' rifles. Lee and her party pretended not to notice and kept walking, but the incident was brought up in a later interrogation when they were asked if their "radio" could reach the United States. Once they were inside the barracks, they heard the door being locked behind them. They were not interned long. Within days, they were encouraged to leave Ecuador. Lee decided en route home that she would never again bring an investor on an expedition!

On another expedition to Ecuador, Lee had leased a magnetometer and a technician to interpret its readings. She was then spending two weeks to a month every January in Ecuador. Lee also hired a boat and captain and divers to participate in her search. The magnetometer technician proved to be dishonest.

The native boat captain noticed that when he passed over known wreck sites, the technician did not report them. Lee also noted spikes on the recorder that the technician discounted as insignificant. That particular expedition was not only disappointing because of the betrayal by the technician, but it was cut short by another of the frequent revolutionary coup d'état disruptions in Ecuador. When the American Embassy in Quito warns that travel is not safe for Americans, it is best to take heed and leave the country.

11

The Avoidance of Boredom

KIM FISHER STAYED SINGLE and focused on the family business for six years after his divorce from Jo. He wondered if any woman could be married to a treasure hunter with all its uncertainties. His mother Dolores was the incredible exception by virtue of her patient devotion to her husband and to her children through the most difficult of financial and emotional times. She was the center of their family strength. Was there a woman in Kim's generation that was his mother's equal? He doubted it. He doubted it so much that he was not searching for a mate.

There is a more compelling reason to treasure hunt than personal wealth. The why in the Fisher family literature is "for the fun, romance, and adventure," but that is only a clue to the state of mind that drives it. Kim simplifies it by saying, "I hate to be bored." Real excitement, the deep kind, cannot be manufactured. It cannot be a mere entertainment. The cure for terminal boredom is a lifelong quest that supersedes every circumstance around it. The quest provides a focus that baffles the terminally satisfied. They do not understand the risks required. They cannot rationalize the persistence after so many documented disappointments.

What kind of brain chemistry happens in the breed of men and women who cannot stand to be bored? Observe them. They are not frenetic in the way that people are nervous and quirky. If they are animated, even to the point of exaggeration, they are yet goal directed. Many of them, like Kim Fisher, are very quiet—people of few words. All the fire is inside, a furnace of determination that you cannot see. And yet the fire is continually there even when the individual appears to be doing nothing. It is as if these explorers know something that we comfort seekers cannot fathom. Do they recognize this flame in each other? Can a man who can't stand to be bored find a woman of the same virtue and make a life together? A wise man once offered this advice about companionship: "First decide where you are going, and then decide who is going with you."

Kim Fisher was only 33 years old when he met Juanita Lee Wiegand in Ecuador. He was much older than his years in experience, and he was committed to being a treasure hunter for the rest of his life. Juanita Lee was a chiropractic doctor with a restless streak. He met her treasure hunting. Did she also dislike being bored?

The Aww Factor

The baby being held by her mother Cheryl and her aunt Dr. Lee Wie-
gand is Stacey Ann Wiley. Grandmother May Wiegand looks on.
The father, Brian, holds the baby's older sister, Sharon, who will grow
up to become the marketing manager of Mel Fisher's Treasures.

ON THE NIGHT OF November 24, 1986, Lee Wiegand, age 31, landed in Philadelphia from a four-day vacation cruise in Cancun and rushed to the Warminster Ambulance Corps station house to keep her 11 p.m. shift duty assignment as an ambulance corps volunteer.

At 2:38 a.m. Lee and the two ambulance corpsmen were dispatched to aid a woman in advanced labor to deliver her second child. Cheryl Wiley had no reason to believe that her baby would come early, but she had had false labor several times that week, so she waited too long that cold, windshield-icy night to wake her husband Brian for the dash to the hospital. Two minutes into the drive, Cheryl knew that she could not delay delivery, and she urged her husband to pull over and seek immediate medical help. In this age before cellphones, Brian had to find an open store to make the emergency call. It was his own business: STAR Lawnmower!

En route to the scene of the call, Lee remarked to the ambulance crew that her younger sister was also expecting her second child. And then reality hit home when Lee recognized the flashing lights of Brian and Cheryl's Toyota. Lee leaped from the ambulance and rushed to her sister's side. Their mother, May, was at Cheryl's house because she had been called to care for the Wileys' two-year-old daughter Sharon.

"Okay," Lee assured her crew, "I've got it."

Lee's confidence was based on eight months spent as a nurse in the delivery room of Doylestown Hospital, her chiropractic doctor degree, and her recent labor-and-birth- delivery retraining through the ambulance paramedic corps. As Cheryl reclined in the passenger seat of the Toyota, her baby's head was already crowning. With the obstetric kit and blankets provided by the ambulance crew, Lee aided her sister in the rapid delivery of Stacey Ann Wiley, 8 pounds, 7 ounces, at 2:50 a.m.

Go ahead. Sigh if you want to. It's a magical family story that appeals to our intuitive natures for empathy. Then, too, you should know that the birth baby's sibling, the then-two-year-old sister Sharon, would grow up to become an important department head in the Kim and Lee Fisher treasure salvage business in Key West.

Considering the emotional content of the unexpected delivery of her sister's baby during an ambulance call, how do you think Lee responds to precious events in other families?

If you are around Lee Fisher in her personal life, you will witness a very expressive, animated woman whose facial reactions mirror her internal emotions. You will also soon be aware that Lee is very empathetic. She listens when you tell her an anecdotal story; and if the event described has an elemental sweetness to it, Lee will respond first by saying, "aww." The word is said as a sigh. It is a universal expression of empathy. The sigh demonstrates understanding and appreciation for what has been shared. It conveys in an instant what otherwise might be lost in the briefness of the personal encounter. And if you could shadow Lee throughout the course of a day when she interacts with family, friends, associates, and employees, you might catch her saying "aww" in response to more than one shared moment of trust and revelation.

Try telling Lee a sentimental story about the birth of a baby or about acquiring a new puppy, and see if you can be the tenth person that week to make her say, "aww." The reaction comes so naturally and so often to her.

14

The Bond of Great Loss

WHEN KIM FISHER AND Lee Wiegand first came together in Ecuador and began to relate as treasure hunters, there came a time when they each had to relate personal stories to further their relationship. At some point as trust was being built, they told each other about both the joys of their past experiences and the deep sense of loss that they had in common. At some point, the sadness and the grief that each felt with having a beloved brother die in a senseless tragedy came up in their conversation. Neither one of them sought to retell the story of their devastating loss, but once acknowledged, the empathy that they could share with each other was a depth of feeling that was generally unavailable to anyone else who had not had the same experience. Few individuals can say in truth, "I understand what you must have felt," unless they have faced the same sacrifice, the same moment of extreme and sudden shock, that seizes the soul-sense of reality.

The Fisher family tragedy came at a time of glorious expectations, and thus its sudden reverse took them to the depths of despair. 1973 is remembered as the first year of finding significant amounts of *Atocha* treasure. After winter storms kept the salvage boats at the dock, the search continued in an area off the Marquesas Keys marked on the charts as The Quicksands, a sandy underwater plateau. The *Southwind*, a converted tugboat captained by the 17-year-old Kim Fisher, could dig a 15-ft. hole in the sand in a few minutes by virtue of its huge 43-inch props. By the middle of May, the *Southwind* was picking up hundreds of pieces-of-eight and then on the 25th, they recovered silver coins by the bucketfuls. They dubbed the discovery area as The Bank of Spain, and it was ultimately to yield over 5,000 coins.

In mid-June, the *Southwind* recovered cannonballs, three rapiers, two swords, a flintlock musket, and nearly 200 silver coins. But Dirk Fisher, age 19, working as a diver on his younger brother's boat while his own command, the *Northwind* converted tug, was sidelined for repairs, made the find of the day. It was a mariner's astrolabe, a ship pilot's most prized navigational device. As only 24 astrolabes survived in world archives, it was considered very valuable. In early July a child's gold rosary with pink coral beads on a 12-inch-long gold chain was found.

But the major find that Fourth of July day was made by Dirk and Kim's younger brother Kane, age 14. As he was searching among a heap of ballast stones that indicated that the hull of a damaged Spanish galleon had split open and spilled its cargo and treasure as it bounced along the bottom, he spied what looked like black loaves of bread at the bottom of a newly blown hole. The loaves proved to be 70 to 90-pound bars of almost pure silver. More importantly, the silver bars had markings that might possibly identify them as the cargo of a specific ship.

On deck in a tank of water, the sulfide tarnish was removed from three of the silver bars to reveal Roman numerals, its mint tally numbers. The bars also showed round tax seals and other shipping markings. While a joyous celebration swept through the Fisher salvage fleet, and the press, including a documentary film crew from the *National Geographic* that recorded it, historian Gene Lyon was in the Key West library examining *Atocha* manifest documents on a microfilm machine. He called the *Southwind* with his exciting news. Silver bar number 4584 was definitely from the *Atocha*! Kim then announced to everyone on deck, "We've got it! The big A. We've found the *Atocha*!"

Subsequently, to silence all critics, the bar was publicly weighed, and it matched the exact weight of 63.60 pounds as recorded on the *Atocha* manifest. The celebration came to the dock in Key West, and its media coverage worldwide set off a reaction that can only be termed "treasure fever."

At the height of public interest that year, Dirk and Angel Curry were married on July 28, 1973, in a storybook wedding held on board the *Golden Doubloon*, a dockside reproduction of a Spanish galleon that served as both a treasure museum and the company offices. Kim served as Dirk's Best Man, and the bridesmaids included Taffi, the brother's younger sister, and Jo Stuart, who was soon to become Kim's wife. Angel, who had originally signed on the treasure hunt as a cook and logbook keeper, then joined the crew of her husband's boat, *Northwind*.

By early 1974, 18-year-old Kim had married Jo in April at her home in Michigan. Unfortunately, the great *Atocha* riches that they discovered and salvaged were not available to the Fisher family because they were tied up in court claims initiated by the State of Florida. Papa Mel sold the remains of his 1715 fleet treasure to pay off bank loans and to pay crew wages and boat expenses to keep the *Atocha* search active. The living was not easy. The family lived in three dilapidated houseboats lashed together along the S. Roosevelt Boulevard bulkhead. Mel, Deo, and Taffi lived in the original one, Dirk and Angel in one, and Kim and Jo in another.

Then in 1982 everything changed for the U.S. treasure salvage industry. The United States Supreme Court ruled against the claims of the State of Florida and U.S. government interests in favor of the Fishers. Funded by a division of their past treasure finds, the *Northwind* and the *Southwind* headed back to the Marquesas. Dirk had recently completed a deep-sea diving school in Fort Lauderdale, so he and Angel were living their dream as young people on a great adventure. On June 12th, Dirk positioned the *Northwind* for an overnight anchoring, but the anchor dragged, so he dove into the water to reset it. At the end of the anchor line, Dirk saw the figure of a cannon—a bronze cannon with dolphin figured lifting rings. Further search uncovered another four before nightfall. Dirk excitedly reported the discovery of the five bronze cannons to headquarters.

Early the next morning Duncan Mathewson, Don Kincaid (photographer), Pat Clyne, and a Channel 4 TV news team rushed to the *Northwind.* Mel and Deo and office staff members arrived the next morning, and Pat Clyne, diving a search pattern, found four additional cannons. Two of the bronze cannons were brought on deck on July 17th. The weight number on one cannon matched that on the *Atocha* gun inventory. Proof positive. Back in Key West with all the media attention, lines of people had gathered at the *Golden Doubloon* to see the *Atocha* cannons. Mel awarded Dirk a $10,000 cash bonus for finding the cannons, and Dirk wasted no time in buying a new car. There were to be no celebratory vacation days, however, as Dirk was anxious to return the *Northwind* to the salvage site.

On July 19th, the *Northwind* left the dock after 2 p.m. and anchored a mile off shore from where its fellow salvage boat, the *Virgalona*, was anchored west of the Marquesas. The day was Angel's birthday so there was a celebration with fried chicken, cake and champagne. Nevertheless, in expectation of a hard workday ahead, "lights out" was called around 11 p.m.

The irony in the deaths of both beloved brothers was that they occurred due to mechanical failures. Even when the circumstances of each catastrophic event is analyzed and the human errors exposed, it seems inappropriate to assign blame. In the equation of accidents, there is no balance between cause and effect that can ever know the consequence of destinies. So much of what happens *in* life *to* life is beyond human control despite our rationalizations to the contrary. We imagine ourselves invincible until loss grips our hearts and proves our vulnerability. Facts have little jurisdiction in the assembly of grief. We, the grieving, are left dumbfounded by the tragic events that penetrate to the depth of our souls. And, always and forever, these accounts of our great loss are painful to retell.

That night on the *Northwind* turned into Sunday, July 20, 1975. Eleven people slept, some in cabins below and others on the deck. Undetected, a rubber hose connection to the boat's toilet came loose, and the 80 p.s.i. water pump that supplied the flushing water system began rapidly flooding the bilge with seawater. The mechanical problem had previously been addressed while the *Northwind* was docked the previous day. A complete new toilet fitting had been installed and the bilge pumped dry. But by best estimates, the fitting worked loose about 3 a.m., and the bilge flooding quietly began.

Many stories of tragedies at sea have ghostly metaphysical elements. In this event Don Kincaid, who was asleep on deck near the pilot house, was awakened close to 5 a.m. by a voice saying, "Hey, look out up there!" Kincaid testified that he saw a figure at the stern rail and heard the voice repeat the warning. Kincaid, still drowsy from sleep, then was aware of the boat's significant list and took immediate action by climbing down to the main deck and waking Donny Jonas, the boat's engineer in charge of pumps. When they checked the engine room, they found to their alarm that it was flooded. Taking emergency action, they shut off the water pumps and opened valves to the fuel tanks to transfer fuel to correct the list, but it was too late. A half-minute later, the *Northwind* rolled over.

Crewmembers sleeping on deck were thrown into the darkness of the water. They included Dirk's youngest brother Kane, age 17, and Angel's 12-year-old brother Keith Curry. Four others in bunkbeds of the crew's quarters below decks had to escape from a dark, upside-down cabin of swirling seawater. Jim Solanick made a miraculous escape through a porthole whose diameter should not have allowed his hips to pass through. Desperation, however, defied the measurement.

Donny Jonas, trapped in the flooded, upside-down engine room, also made a death-defying escape as he found a waterproof flashlight and figured out an underwater passage to a hatch. Survivors from the deck who were clinging to the upturned bottom of the hull could hear Jonas pleading for help as he struggled to find a way to the surface.

When a long cushion from a deck lounge chair surfaced, the seven older survivors put Keith, the boy, in the makeshift raft that was also kept afloat by two life jackets, two Styrofoam ball-shaped lobster pot buoys, and two inflated plastic bags. Sunrise was still more than an hour away as the survivors clung to their improvised raft as it drifted away from the overturned *Northwind*.

All were painfully aware that Dirk, Angel, and diver Rick Gage, had not surfaced from their cabins below deck.

Captain Demostines "Mo" Molinar on the *Virgalona* noticed in the light of day that the *Northwind* was gone from its night anchorage. He assumed that Dirk had begun salvage operations early. As the *Virgalona* got underway toward the operational area, the crew caught sight of young Keith Curry kneeling on the makeshift raft and waving a flashlight to get their attention. Later, when the *Virgalona* located the sunken *Northwind*, divers were deployed to retrieve the bodies while the survivors watched. The family of young adventurers was thus driven to a depth of emotions that few have experienced.

That Sunday morning, Mel and Deo had spent the night at the Pier House following the weekend-long celebration of the bronze cannons find. When they were reached, they were told that there had been an accident at sea, but they only learned about the deaths at the Coast Guard station. Their loss was so devastating to the entire Fisher family that many believed that Dirk and Angel's deaths would end the company's search for the remainder of the *Atocha*'s treasure.

When Kim and Lee talked about their families, and specifically about their brothers, during their first meeting in Ecuador in 1986, the tragic death of Lee's brother Scott was still painfully recent. First Lieutenant Michael Scott Wiegand, U.S. Air Force, at age 26, a jet fighter pilot instructor, was killed on January 11, 1985, when a mechanical failure caused his jet aircraft to dive out of control into the barren desert near Albuquerque, New Mexico. The news of his violent, unexpected death did not reach the Wiegand family until the following day, January 12th, which concurred with Kim's birthday. Thus, in celebrating one life, the loss of another is brought back into memory. Wounds, although aged by scars, are yet sensitive to the touch of anniversaries.

Scott, as the son of a career Navy pilot, grew up in a military family. His father Victor had risen to the rank of Commander and had seen wartime service. Imagine the family pride when Scott got his Air Force wings as an officer pilot. Scott's three sisters—Juanita Lee, Jacqueline, and Cheryl—must have gushed over him when he appeared in uniform at family holiday parties. Then, too, Robert, a successful chiropractor, was also glad for his dashing younger brother's achievement. Vic and May Wiegand could not have been happier for the prospects of their five children. Then, in the most tragic and unexpected way, their family portrait was shattered on a most unforgettable January day.

The official Air Force declarations of the accident that killed their son and brother were very devastating to the Wiegand family. There were really no causative details. Scott was on a routine solo flight, and something indeterminate went terribly wrong. The fighter jet nosed over and dove into the desert, instantly killing the pilot. In the complex technical world of military aviation, accidents occur that are sometimes unexplainable, the Wiegand family was told. There was no evidence of pilot error.

The gnawing feeling of indetermination in the accident report of Scott's death lasted for ten years before it was brought to an unofficial dramatic conclusion. One day a stranger came to Vic and May's door and asked to speak privately with them. He was a retired enlisted-rank Air Force aircraft mechanic and had come to confess to the Wiegands his role in Scott's death. For his own fearful reasons, he had kept secret his unrelenting guilt until he was out of the Air Force. Conscience, however, compelled him to locate the parents of the pilot that he felt he had condemned to death by an aircraft repair oversight. The schedule on the flight line had been demanding, he told them. He was tired and frustrated when he released Scott's jet for duty. He should have checked one more of the plane's mechanical problem areas, but he let it ride. When he learned that witnesses on the ground reported that Scott's jet made a sudden nosedive without the hope of correction, he said that he knew the cause to be his dereliction of duty on the flight line. He, obviously, had not reported his conclusions to the Air Force accident investigators.

The sincere contrition of the retired Air Force mechanic moved Vic and May to express their Christian charity. After all, they had participated in Navy chapel programs as choir members and Sunday School teachers at every posting during Vic's career. Then, too, who knew more the vicissitudes of military life? Who knew more than Vic that many dangers in military service occur by chance and are beyond anyone's control? Was the penitent guilty of gross negligence that cost a comrade his life? It was not an intentional act, but rather one of omission. Whatever the truthful circumstances, the Wiegands would not condemn the man, and he was allowed to part with their gentle benediction.

It is in the telling of our most personal stories to each other that we bond in mutual trust and even in admiration. In sharing great loss is born empathy that has as its natural consequence the feelings of love.

The Proposal

IN THE YEARS SINCE their initial Ecuadorian adventure, Kim and Lee had had romantic rendezvous on an irregular basis, but they had not yet come together as a committed couple. Marriage was something that neither one of them required from the other. Individually, their independence from conventional expectations had been hard won, and thus any radical change from their liberated lifestyles was rationally inconceivable.

Lee had no presumptions of permanent coupling when she scheduled a month of treasure diving on the *Atocha* wreck site with Kim. There was the promise of their mutual affections, and the renewal of friendships with Mel, Deo, and the Fisher family, but Lee's practical life was still rooted in Pennsylvania. No matter how wonderful her vacation days were in Key West, Lee had no further designs on Kim.

Kim thought that he was steering the same uncommitted course as Lee, but after she returned to Pennsylvania, questions and feelings began to emerge that startled him. Whenever he thought about Lee, he experienced a "hollow spot" in his chest. He then asked himself, "Am I ever going to commit to a companion for the rest of my life? Is Lee the one?" The questions were persistent.

Then that week, Coast Guard authorities asked Kim to use his boat and side-scan sonar to locate a downed small civilian aircraft that had crashed in Florida Bay. Someone's hopes and plans had come to an abrupt and final end.

Out on the ocean, Kim could not prevent thoughts about his own mortality. The years were passing quickly, and although he

The bride and groom with her parents Vic and May Wiegand

enjoyed financial success and a measure of even fame, he felt an unfulfilled dimension in his life. It was decision time. Could he allow Lee to walk away, or would he take action?

The action that he took began at the Key West shop of the famous emerald jewelry designer Manuel Marcial of Emeralds International. "Make me an emerald engagement ring, and make it today." Friends make the impossible happen, and Kim had the custom-made ring within 24 hours.

Kim's next affirmative act was to send Lee a dozen long-stemmed red roses to her apartment in Bucks County, PA. The flowers arrived as a mystery. The card must have been lost in delivery, so neither Lee nor her roommate knew the sender. Lee admits that she did not consider that they came from Kim. In fact, she thanked her date that night for the flowers. He responded in a sullen tone, "They are not from me."

Later, Kim called to say, "I have something that I need to talk to you about." He had booked a flight to Philadelphia, and Lee agreed to meet him at the airport. Lee says that she thought that Kim wanted to discuss another treasure hunting expedition. Really. She was also surprised that Kim had wanted to follow her to Pennsylvania after only two days apart, but she did not leap to romantic conclusions.

During the 45-minute drive from the airport to her apartment, Lee remembers that Kim talked incessantly, which seemed odd to her. She had never seen him so talkative. Neither one of them remembers the content. Back at her apartment, it was about 1 a.m. when Lee said to Kim, "I need to get some sleep. I have to see patients at 9 a.m."

Kim then responded, "I have a question. Will you marry me?"

Lee was so shocked that she could only ask, "What?"

Kim then repeated his proposal. "Would you marry me?" And then from behind his back, he brought forward the beautiful emerald engagement ring.

Lee says that she paused for no more than two seconds before saying, "Yes, I will marry you." The ring when placed on Lee's finger fit perfectly.

At age 34, with so much hard-won independence behind her, saying yes to an unexpected marriage proposal was a tremendous leap of both love and faith for Lee. Of course, there was the history of their romantic adventures together and Kim's striking good looks, but some members of Lee's family seriously doubted that she would ever judge any man good enough to marry. Imagine the surprise of Lee's parents when she brought Kim to meet them the next evening after her workday.

Lee introduced Kim, and in the same motion, she held up her ring hand to flash the emerald announcement of their engagement. Kim then by tradition asked the navy commander permission to marry his daughter.

"Do you love her?" her father Vic asked.

"Yes, I do," Kim answered.

Then to Lee, he asked the same question. "Yes," she said, "I love him."

"Then you have my permission."

The proposal happened about 1 a.m. on a Saturday morning. The church wedding with bridesmaids, groomsmen, flowers, special music, and a 200-guest reception at the naval officers club took place the following Saturday, June 10, 1989. The Fisher family, including Mel and Dolores, flew in from Key West. Those readers who have ever planned a wedding know that you absolutely cannot pull off anything like what Lee and her family did in one week. And yet, everywhere that Lee turned, people said yes and made the impossible happen.

A former nurse, Lee got an immediate appointment for the required blood test. A clerk cooperated with a one-stop marriage license. Lee's female Presbyterian minister, performing June weddings by the dozen, opened the church for a 6 p.m. candlelight ceremony followed by a one-hour wedding photo session.

Church policy required a marriage counseling class prior to a wedding, so Lee and Kim made an appointment. After asking them to pledge their love for each other, the minister released them in the space of a few minutes. Kim and the groomsmen went for tuxedo fittings while Lee turned her bridesmaids loose in a shopping mall. Her only instruction was for them to buy matching cocktail-length dresses that they would want to wear again. Lee's father was concerned about finding all the accoutrements to his Naval officer's dress-white uniform with sword, but those details came together, too.

Meanwhile, from day one, Lee's mother May and her sisters Jacqueline and Cheryl went through Lee's address book and made telephone calls to friends and family. On less than a week's notice, a church full of people promised to attend.

The bride and groom with his parents Mel and Deo Fisher

The biggest concern to every bride is, of course, "the" dress. The wedding gown must capture her most beautiful moment. Some brides spend weeks looking at bridal dresses in bride magazines, and then shop for weeks to find the garment that her mother and sisters will agree is perfect for her. Lee needed a miracle to find her wedding gown. The miracle came in a box labeled as a sample dress. Dresses destined for display on mannequins are always size nine. Lee is a size nine. The sample dress in the box was both wonderful and perfect fitting. The store owner released it. The mannequin could wait.

While admiring Lee in her wedding dress and knowing of her adventurous life style, the store owner suggested a crowning touch for her trip down the aisle. For both the style and character of the bride, the store owner produced a buccaneer-styled lacy wedding hat. Lee was very pleased by the addition of the hat because she knew how surprised and happy it would make Kim when he saw it. The pirate look was favored by both of them, and it would later be costumed to perfection as the couple represented the romance of treasure hunting to the members of Mel Fisher's Expeditions.

15

The Underwater Wedding

WHEN WE CONSIDER THE Fisher family adventure odyssey that revolves around love and treasure, its grandest metaphor may well be an underwater wedding. Today, romantic dive partners can book underwater wedding packages in the Florida Keys, Mexico, Bali and Bora Bora in the Pacific, and even in China and Russia. But in June 1990, the staging of an underwater wedding was a unique first-time event that attracted national television coverage.

The groom, Jacques Lemaire, born of French and Belgian parents, was an adventurer who had flown crop dusters in Morocco, lost his sailboat in a storm off South Africa, and then captained a 130-ft. three-masted top sail schooner, the *Aquila Marina*, owned by Jochen Mass, the German Grand Prix racecar driver who was sponsored by Anheuser-Busch. The classic sailboat sailed the Caribbean and up and down the U.S. coast from Florida to Maine at the convenience of its owner and sponsor. All this before Jacques arrived in Key West in his mid-40s.

The bride, Terrie Thorbjornson, was from a seafaring family on the coast of Maine, and it was she who suggested that the couple locate Mel Fisher and get into the lifestyle of treasure

hunting. The couple had met on St. Thomas in the Virgin Islands when Jacques came to Underwater Safaris, a dive shop where Terrie worked, to rent equipment for night dives off the *Aquila Marina*. Captain Jacques used his prerogative to make Terrie, the beautiful Swede, his dive buddy. The law of natural attraction took its course, but the romance was then cut short when the great schooner sailed away to another port.

Jacques Lemaire and Terrie Thorbjornson near their underwater wedding day

Fate, however, intervened. It was 1986, and the remaining tall ships of sailing history were gathered in New York harbor to celebrate the 100th anniversary of the Statue of Liberty. Terrie arrived as cook and crewmember of the *Western Star*, a boat owned by her boss at the St. Thomas dive shop. When they reached their assigned anchorage, the boat anchored nearest to them was the *Aquila Marina*. Jacques and Terrie were happily reunited, and Terrie spent all of her free time on the schooner where the party seemed non-stop. When her employer strongly objected to her liberal behavior, Terrie says that she "jumped ship." She put all her personal belongings quickly into plastic trash bags and joined Jacques on the *Aquila Marina*. The couple worked the majestic schooner for two years before making the decision to come to Key West and become treasure hunters.

When Dr. Lee Wiegand, the adventurous chiropractor from Pennsylvania, arrived in Key West for a month-long treasure hunting adventure, Mel assigned her to Kim Fisher's boat the *Bookmaker*, a converted 42-foot Hatteras, now outfitted for treasure salvaging. Jacques and Terrie were the crew. Jacques was the first mate, and Terrie was the cook. Both were scuba certified, and both had already felt the thrill of finding treasure. Lee's presence on the *Bookmaker* then made the boat a two-couple operation.

Terrie says, "I could just tell. There was chemistry between them. And maybe I pushed a little bit, because I liked Lee, and I wanted to see them together. So I made candlelight dinners for them on the back deck, and Jacques and I were mindful to give them their personal space. Lee was a breath of fresh air, as far as we were concerned. She was smart, enthusiastic, and she had led an adventurous life similar to ours. She was one of us, and we recognized it."

Evidently, Kim recognized it, too. Within 48 hours of Lee returning to Pennsylvania, he followed her and proposed marriage as he presented her with a large *Atocha* emerald engagement ring. They were married the following Saturday, June 10, 1989. Lee then came home to Key West and went back to treasure hunting on the *Bookmaker* as Kim's wife and crewmember. The *Bookmaker* was definitely a "love boat" as crewed by its two romantic couples.

In addition to their work on the *Bookmaker*, the two couples toured for seven years together with the *Atocha* treasures during the winter off-season where their sale of coins and other artifacts helped to underwrite the expenses of the company's continuing salvage operations.

Almost a year had passed since Kim and Lee's wedding when Jacques and Terrie contemplated doing the same. No one remembers exactly how the idea of an underwater wedding emerged. Terrie speculates with humor that it was probably hatched one night at Sloppy Joe's, a favorite Key West watering hole. Whenever it was, the concept gained immediate support, and everyone in the Fisher organization wanted in on the planning. It was very natural for the newly wedded Kim and Lee to support a special wedding day for their friends and shipmates, considering Terrie and Jacques's role in their romantic courtship.

Don Kincaid, retired from the company after going to sea with the Fishers since 1971, offered his newly built spacious sailing catamaran, *The Stars & Stripes*, as the principal wedding party dive boat and reception platform. The chosen site for the nuptials was off Sand Key, a 45-minute boat ride out of Key West. A flotilla of boats carried the wedding party and guests to the location. Terrie remembers that there were so many divers in the shallow waters selected for the ceremony that the film crews asked them to remove their fins. Their swimming was stirring up sand and clouding the water.

The excitement of the underwater wedding somehow attracted the CBS News network television show *48 Hours*, and the producers sent a crew to document the event. Jacques remembers the Persian Gulf War news compromising everything else on television when Iraq invaded Kuwait on August 2nd, so the national audience for their underwater wedding was not what it might have been. Pat Clyne, however, shot and produced his own video of the event that became a treasured keepsake.

What kind of minister do you get to perform the ceremony for an underwater wedding? The Fishers had to look no further than their executive office where Mel's administrative assistant, Judy Sojourner (Gracer), was a Notary Public and qualified to legally bind the couple in matrimony. Over her years with the company, Judy had officiated in about fifteen weddings for divers, including Captain Andy Matroci, Mel's daughter Taffi, and even the daughters of the company's corporate attorneys, albeit on dry land.

For the Jacques and Terrie ceremony, Judy outfitted herself in scuba gear, with a slate and grease pencil to write instructions to the bride and groom. The most important note on the slate read, "Say I do." When Pat Clyne came to edit his video of the underwater wedding, he realized that he needed to add the dramatic sound of Judy's voice. In the studio, Judy voiced-over her instructions as if she were speaking through her scuba mouthpiece. The trick was performed by using her index finger to vibrate her lips to simulate talking underwater.

Tom Ford, a diver and then boat captain who had been present for both the tragic event of 1975 and the recovery of the *Atocha* Mother Lode in 1985, held the lightly weighted Judy in place for the ceremony while Greta, Tom's wife, swam nearby in a mermaid costume. Judy remembers the bride and groom approaching her through an archway of raised spear guns. The underwater direction of the wedding ceremony was overtaken by the *48 Hours* CBS film crew who hovered in the water and gave instructional hand signals. Pat Clyne, who for years had documented the entire Fisher family treasure odyssey on film, shot his footage independent of the CBS crew.

Jacques and Terrie's underwater ceremony occurred on June 7th, a few days short of the first anniversary of Kim and

Lee's wedding. The two couples shared many memorable years treasure hunting on the *Bookmaker*. Eventually the time came for Kim and Lee to come off the water and into the office to learn the operational end of the business.

Kim tutored under Mel for the salvage end, which included the fleet of company boats and crew, subcontractors' boats and crews, contracts, getting expedition members, doing PR, and many other CEO duties. Lee dove into the retail end of the business, bringing the skills that she had learned from seven years of touring with the treasures through the finest jewelry stores in America and Canada.

When Kim and Lee left the *Bookmaker*, Jacques was given command of the boat, and he and Terrie continued to treasure hunt for nearly ten more years. Jacques considers their time in Key West with the Fishers to be the best years of his life with all the romance and adventure.

Jacques says, "It was a sweet life."

16

The Admiral

WHEN THE NEWLY MARRIED Lee Fisher came to Key West to join the family treasure operations, she fit in to the salvage boat team as a certified diver. One day at sea, where her primary job was magging to find new targets to salvage, Lee was on the stern of Kim's 42-ft. Hatteras, the *Bookmaker*, which had been converted into a workboat. Lee was tossing cinder block-weighted buoys into the water each time the magnetometer indicated a hit below. The job of preparing and throwing buoys in the hot sun made Lee wonder what her title might be among the crewmembers. Previously, in her chiropractic practice, she had been called "Doctor." On board the salvage boat, where Mel was the king of the Conch Republic, and Kim a captain, and crewmembers had titles like chief engineer, master diver, and cook, what was she?

When Mel approached her on the stern deck that day, Lee could not help herself from asking, "Dad," she said, "everyone on the boat has a title but me. Kim's the captain, Jacques is first mate, and Terrie is the cook. What am I?"

Without skipping a heartbeat, Mel replied, "Why you're the Admiral, of course."

Lee's mates on the *Bookmaker* overheard that conversation, and her new title stuck.

Being called "Admiral" was an especially meaningful sobriquet because Lee's father Vic had had a long career in the U.S. Navy as a commander. The fact that Mel could spontaneously give Lee the inside-family title of "admiral" was typical of his sensitivity and intelligence as a social activator. Mel Fisher could not only charm gold, silver, and emeralds off a sea bottom; he could also give those around him a sense of importance.

Kim, although a captain and the CEO of Mel Fisher's Treasures, will say that his wife as "the admiral" outranks him. It is an inside-family joke, but those whom Mel Fisher has knighted with his conch shell scepter, shall ever retain their titles.

17

Touring with the Atocha Treasures

IN CITIES ACROSS AMERICA, people who learned about the amazing treasure of gold, silver and emeralds, the *Atocha's* Mother Lode, wanted to see it. Many of them had seen the treasure brought up by divers on *National Geographic* television specials or in the extensive pictorial magazine feature articles. Some of them had read one of the six major books that described in detail the 16-year-long effort to locate the famous 1622 Spanish galleon. Whatever the depth of their knowledge, a lot of people wanted to see the *Atocha* treasures as much as they did the King Tut exhibition that was touring major American museums.

Whether you went to see the *Atocha* treasures or the King Tut ancient Egyptian artifacts, you may have had to stand in line for anywhere from two to four hours. For the *Atocha* experience, you might be out in the cold at freestanding exhibition locations or foot weary on the concourses of a mall. The wait may have been long, but the show was worth it. In mall areas outside of the exhibition jewelry stores, the Fisher road company erected a stage with a screen where archaeologist Jim Sinclair could tell the *Atocha* story and where Pat Clyne could illustrate it with a color slide show. Often without permits of any kind, the little theatre on the mall erected by the Fisher crew spontaneously appeared and disappeared within a period of three days. The road show production required 50 trunks of display props, audiovisual equipment, *Atocha* artifacts, and team member clothing.

Once inside the exhibit, visitor expectations were rewarded, and an air of excitement was communicated. The infectious Caribbean melodies of Jimmy Buffett and Harry Belafonte filled the air, and the Fisher crew was dressed for Key West in colorful short-sleeve shirts, shorts, and sandals. Each wore his or her own Key West "dog-tag"—an *Atocha* coin hanging from a neck chain. Life is a beach that we want to share with you, they seemed to say.

"The only thing lacking in the atmosphere that we set," Lee says, "is the salt sea smell of the ocean. Maybe we should have brought in baskets of seaweed."

Once inside the exhibit, visitors were allowed to heft a heavy silver ingot and hold a solid gold bar. The 80-pound silver ingot, too difficult to ship reliably to the next exhibition stop, was carried by a crewmember in a piece of hand luggage that was often put in the overhead compartment of a commercial aircraft. Gold jewelry, emeralds, and other *Atocha* artifacts considered too valuable or too fragile to ship were also carried by team members. Traveling to shows in Canada presented an amusing security problem when custom agents opened team members' hand luggage to expose a priceless cache of treasures. Their awe and excitement was vocal, and it attracted unwanted attention to the Americans as customs agents gathered to marvel at the *Atocha* riches.

The setup for the traveling *Atocha* exhibit and artifact sale was to contract with a guild-level jewelry store to remove all its diamond rings, Rolex watches, and other valuables from its display cases, so that the Fishers could replace them with historic artifacts and certified *Atocha* items for sale. The authentic gold bars, cups, and silver ingots, the Muzo emeralds, and the silver pieces-of-eight on display were alone valued in the tens of millions of dollars.

The Fisher road team included Kim and Lee, security guards, and a sales team of nine people who could talk history and adventure and then sell certified *Atocha* coins and other artifact items to the excited crowd who wanted to own a piece of history.

"We wanted the display counters lined with our people," Lee said. "We had to show and tell and sell to keep the crowd of people moving through the store. Lunches, and even bathroom breaks, were hard to come by. With setup hours we worked 15-hour days, mostly on our feet. Suppertime, if you could find a restaurant open, would often come after 10:30 at night. Then we all went to our hotel rooms and flopped into bed. Although we often had a $100,000-plus sales day, we were too tired to celebrate. The next morning, we had to be up early to groom ourselves for another long day of meeting the public and responding cheerfully and professionally to their questions."

The tour schedule for seven years in the early 1990s was extensive. Shreve & Company, Jewelers Since 1852, with locations on Michigan Avenue in Chicago and on Grant Avenue in San Francisco, among other locations, sent formal invitations to its best customers. The invitation was to attend "an exclusive private showing," a "Museum quality showing" of *Atocha* artifacts at a reception where cocktails and hors d'oeuvres would be served. This privileged clientele would meet firsthand "Expedition

Leader" Captain Kim Fisher and archaeologist James Sinclair and not only view slides of the actual undersea discovery but also have the first opportunity to buy the "many millions of dollars of this treasure for sale." The reception was scheduled an evening prior to the four-day "limited time only" offering to the public. How could one resist being part of such an event?

In locations as distant as the Hawaii Jewelry Design Center in Honolulu and Reeds Jewelers in Savannah, Georgia, the three and four-day exhibition and sale events went on. Own a piece of history. Authentic shipwreck treasure. One-of-a-kind treasure jewelry. Meet the world's greatest treasure hunter. One of the greatest adventurers of our time. *Atocha* treasure: gold, silver, and emerald jewelry, coins each with a certificate of authenticity. Museum quality re-creations of *Atocha* artifacts fashioned from the galleon's gold and silver cargo. The invitations, postcards, flyers, banners, and announcements spelled it out.

Behind the scenes, the company produced a sales associate guide to the merchandise selections available for sale during the traveling exhibitions. Printed in 1995, the 8 1/2 x 11, 24-page booklet summarized the age of *Atocha* in historic terms, the Mel Fisher personal story of finding the *Atocha* that established him as the "World's Greatest Treasure Hunter," and even the court battles that ended with a landmark decision in the U.S. Supreme Court that finally granted the Fisher family complete ownership of the *Atocha* wreck and its treasures.

Sections of the booklet are then devoted to identifying genuine *Atocha* treasure coins known as "Pieces of Eight," the minted silver Spanish Real, *Atocha* emeralds, and the Renaissance Fine Jewelry Collection that included The Maltese Cross, Olive Blossom Chains in gold or silver, a wide variety of rings, and other unique items related to the *Atocha*. The detailed history and description of each item provided talking points when a customer showed interest. The instruction booklet demonstrated that every item in the sale had a unique story behind it.

The reach of the *Atocha* story into popular American culture is pervasive. Christie's, the famed Park Avenue New York City auction house, exhibited a selection of the finest items from the *Atocha* and *Santa Margarita* at their showrooms in Geneva, London, Amsterdam, Tokyo, and Caracas during the spring of 1988. The Christie's catalog for the subsequent auction called it, "the most spectacular shipwreck sale in history and without doubt the largest dispersal of treasure ever held." The sale itself was held on June 14th and 15th. Artifacts on the block included a "superb two-handled gold wine cup from the *Atocha*" estimated to bring $120,000 to $180,000; a 62-inch gold chain estimated at $150,000 to $250,000; a coral and gold rosary at $150,000 to $250,000; a large emerald set in a gold ring at $40,000 to $60,000; silver dinner plates at $2,000 to $3,000 each; and a silver-gilt rosewater dish at $80,000 to $120,000. The offering also included 50 silver bars weighing 60 to 70 pounds each, four navigator's astrolabes, two-escudo gold coins, other gold and silver coins, small gold chains, and a finely-enameled emerald-set of studs for a gentleman's shirt.

In reviewing the public fascination with the shipwreck treasures recovered by the Fisher family, the company archives contain many of the hundreds of magazine feature stories, newspaper reports, and filmed documentaries for television, but certainly not all. Among the oddities of all the media attention over a period of more than 40 years, two demonstrate the scope of the coverage.

The first is a 2006 feature segment on the *Jay Leno* late-night television show. Mo Rocca, a thin, bespeckled, comedic master of the ridiculous-interview genre, visits Kim and Pat Clyne in Key West to "report" on the treasure fever phenomena. Mo briefly does the maritime museum tour and then poses with gold chains around his neck in a way that resembles a Woody Allen posture expressing both joy and bewilderment. Mo is playing everything for laughs until he goes to sea with Kim on the *Magruder* and suits up in dive gear. He attempts to cover his deep-water fear of *Jaws* by nervously cavorting with the barechested manly *Magruder* crew. The gags continue as Mo goes underwater with Kim and finds Sponge Bob Square Pants from the cartoon show on the *Atocha* shipwreck site. And what luck. Mo finds a bar of gold!

Back on deck, Mo leads the salvage boat crew in a chorus line dance that only goes to prove what great sports they are to support Mo in his mockery of news reporting. The comedy spot from 2006 continues to live as thousands of new viewers discover it as a YouTube video. And despite the slapstick nature of Mo Rocca's comedy, seeing Kim, Pat, and the treasure hunters having fun is well worth watching.

Another more esoteric find in the Fisher company archives that demonstrates the breadth of its cultural scope appears in the June 2011 edition of *In Style Magazine*. On page 68, in a section titled "The Look We're Loving," the Academy Award-winning actress Halle Berry is pictured wearing a Robert Rodriguez wrap dress and one of the *Atocha*'s silver coins designed into a diamond-studded sterling silver chain from Irit Design. An insert photo shows the detail of the coin at the end of the chain. Even if you are Halle Berry, the *Atocha* coin on display around your neck is a guaranteed conversation piece, and the history behind it is exciting to tell.

18

The Beale Treasure

MORE THAN A FEW excited individuals try to reach Kim Fisher each year with treasure maps and claims of great riches to be discovered. They offer the company a split on anything found, but they never offer to put up any financial capital in the treasure search. They expect the Fisher company to finance the entire expedition, take all the risks, and provide all the expertise and equipment. Mel, too, had people frequently approach him with treasure location schemes. One of the most bizarre of these treasure stories launched Mel on a rare land hunt—a rapid deployment of resources and crew to locate The Beale Treasure.

In the Blue Ridge Mountains of western central Virginia near the Blue Ridge Parkway is Bedford county and Goose Creek at Graham's Mill. Legend insists that Thomas Jefferson Beale and his partners buried 5,100 pounds of silver; 2,921 pounds of gold; and a large fortune in precious jewels in the Bedford area in 1820. The Beale party left behind a three-part code based on the Declaration of Independence that is said to reveal the exact location of the treasure "packed in iron pots with iron covers in a burial vault roughly lined with stone." If true, the legend again proves that truth is often stranger than fiction. And evidently enough people believe the Beale Treasure story to attract treasure hunters from all over the world who constantly dig up Bedford county and benefit the tourist economy of Bedford, the nearest town with restaurants and accommodations.

In 1989, a Sarasota, Florida woman is reported to have contacted Mel and told him that she had broken parts of the Beale Treasure code. For one-third of the treasure, she gave Mel these key words from the code: *cave, falls, elbow, hub, creek,* and *hole.* Mel then sold one-percent shares for $20,000 each and one-quarter of one-percent shares for $5,000 to finance one year of the hunt through December 31, 1990. In September 1989, Mel visited the Goose Creek site and declared, "As soon as I saw it, I knew this was it." A newspaper reported that he then purchased the five and one-half acre property from the owners for a reported $50,000 plus a one-percent share.

Mel and Kim in the Virginia mountains on the Beale Treasure site

Lee remembers the rush to Bedford County, Virginia to dig for the Beale Treasure as a complete surprise. The assembled search team included her, Mel, Kim, and videographer Pat Clyne, and a local contractor and crew who had been hired to move tons of silt around the Graham's Mill dam. Mel believed that Beale had diverted Goose Creek at the mill, buried the treasure, and then returned the creek to its normal course. When it was learned that Mel, the famous treasure hunter, was digging for the Beale fortune, the media from Roanoke, Richmond, and Washington, D.C. descended on the site with reporters and major network television crews. Even a *National Geographic* film crew came to shoot documentary footage. As if the painful labor in the muddy work site were not enough, the tree-lined hillside overlooking the treasure site was always packed with onlookers. Poor Lee, like all the men on the crew, had to find a place behind a tree or vehicle where she could change clothes and relieve herself camp style.

Then, to complicate the treasure-digging circus, local, state, and federal officials appeared to enforce applicable regulations. The county of Bedford required a permit for sediment control. The Virginia State Water Control Board and the Army Corps of Engineers demanded that a plan be submitted as to how to prevent the erosion of land into the creek. The Fisher crew was also reprimanded for not wearing hard hats in and around the primary dig site.

The dig had started after the creek had been diverted below the dam, with Kim and Lee doing the major shovel work. When the hole reached a depth of four feet, and they were near exhaustion, a backhoe was hired, and the hole expanded until it swallowed the backhoe, and a much larger piece of earth-moving equipment—a track hoe—was employed with a local operator behind the wheel. The excavation then grew to the size of a deep quarry. As the hole deepened, it had to be examined with the metal detector, a heavy electric wand on a 150-foot cable attached to two large truck batteries. Lee recalls handling the daily movements of the metal detector as hard, cold, and muddy labor.

The Fishers were approached multiple times by many of the local bystanders who advised them in a Virginia mountaineer twang that they were digging in the wrong place. It seems that lots of Bedford county hill people had positions on where the Beale Treasure was buried; and for a price, or a share, they were willing to divulge it. Lee and Kim followed one convincing local on a steep mountain climb to reach an observation point. The man pointed across a valley to a rocky outcropping and advised them to dig there. They had to then wonder if they had been the victims of a practical joke. Maybe there was a local merchant conspiracy to keep the treasure hunters digging, especially famous ones like Mel Fisher, who attracted a horde of media and onlookers to fill their motels, restaurants, hardware stores, and shops.

After a frantic month of earth moving, activity at the mill site came to an abrupt halt on Wednesday, the day before Thanksgiving. The gate to the treasure site was locked and a "No Trespassing" sign posted. There was no sign of Mel, his family, or his crew. Mel finally appeared late that afternoon at a Richmond television station to explain. He said that his crew had located three empty vaults during their time on the site, and he felt that the treasure had been moved. With snow falling and the weather worsening, he and his family had decided to spend the holidays and the remainder of the winter back in the warmer climates of Florida and the Caribbean where they had many ongoing salvage operations.

Lee remembers that she and Kim were happy to quit the Virginia mountains and Mel's land quest for The Beale Treasure. Legends and secret codes are better left to action-adventure filmmakers, they thought. Better the documented history of shipwreck manifests to pursue in familiar seas.

19

The Treasure Catalog

Ask any captain or crewmember on a Fisher expedition treasure salvage boat why they persist in going to sea year after year, and they will respond in the same way. It is the lure of adventure.

"You never know from one diving day to the next what will be recovered," they say.

Since the *Atocha* Mother Lode was found in July 1985 as the richest Spanish galleon ever salvaged to date, the search for the equally valuable sterncastle of the *Atocha* has continued with a much lesser degree of media attention. And yet, amazing artifacts are still being found as the *Atocha* and *Santa Margarita* Spanish galleon shipwreck sites continue to be searched.

On April 11, 2008, diving on a *Santa Margarita* site, 16,184 pearls were found in a damaged lead box. The pearls had blackened after 386 years on the ocean bottom, and they resembled an assortment of BBs. It took John Corcoran, senior conservator at Mel Fisher's Treasures, ten months to restore the pearls to their original luster. The value of the 251 largest and highest quality of these pearls had an estimated market value of more than $3 million. The biggest pearl, some 52 carats, was viewed as one of the largest pearls in the world and was valued at nearly $500,000. All this considerable treasure went into that year's expedition member Division.

In March 2011, a 40-inch, 55-link gold chain was another late *Atocha* recovery. Its estimated value, as reported by *Forbes Magazine*, was $250,000. Then in late June of the same year, an ancient gold ring with a 10-carat square-cut emerald was recovered with silver spoons and other silver artifacts. The ring alone was initially valued at $500,000 as reported by NBC's Channel 6 in South Florida.

In the fall of 2000, Atocha Treasure Tours, Inc. published a first-edition mail-order catalog that featured original artifacts from the *Atocha* including gold and silver bars, jewelry coins, emeralds, original rings and merchandise from their museum gift shops. The full-color magazine format 52-page publication was titled *Discovery Day Treasures*. The catalog is of special interest because it combines all the colorful elements of the Fisher family story with photographs and prices of the treasures that were then available to the public. The premiere item is a gold and emerald broach from the *Atocha* offered at $1,100,000. An elaborate gold spoon with an Indian face from the *Atocha* is offered at $560,000. A 1622 bar of gold is listed at $76,000. A plumed warrior gold gentleman's toothpick on a gold mesh chain from the 1715 Spanish Treasure Fleet is priced at $235,000. Not your average mail-order catalog, is it?

For documentarians and collectors of Fisher family memorabilia, the catalog offers reminders of the extensive exposure generated by *National Geographic* feature magazine articles and films. The first article appeared in June 1976 after the discovery of the *Atocha* bronze cannons, and a second in February 1982 as the treasure trail continued to produce valuable artifacts. Don Kincaid, a vice-president of Treasure Salvors at the time, provided photography for the magazines and for the later *National Geographic* television film documentary. The feature article, "Santa Margarita: Treasure from the Ghost Galleon" was written by Eugene Lyon, the historian and archivist whose research helped the Fishers locate both the *Santa Margarita* and the *Atocha*.

A third *National Geographic* feature had documented the recovery of the 1715 Spanish fleet treasures when Mel first came to Florida and teamed his group with the boats and crews of Kip Wagner. Then following the recovery of *Atocha*'s Mother Lode in 1985, the Geographic Society produced a second documentary for television titled,

Atocha: Quest for Treasure. These magazine features and highly rated television showings of the Fisher salvors in action generated worldwide interest that continues to the present day.

Hollywood cashed in on the Fisher success story in the television film *Dreams of Gold*, released in November 1986, starring Cliff Robertson as Mel and Loretta Swit as Deo. The film is still available on DVD, and its trailer can be viewed on YouTube. The movie is offered in the catalog in a DVD format for $19.95.

Pictured in the catalog is a bust of Mel sculpted by Don Wiegand. Mel is shown in the prime of his discovery years, a mature man in eyeglasses wearing a heavy gold chain and a silver piece-of-eight on a chain as proof of his *Atocha* finds. The inscription reads, "In Memoriam, Mel Fisher, 1922-1998, The World's Greatest Treasure Hunter." It can be seen in the Mel Fisher Maritime Heritage Museum and also in the company's current executive office. The memorial page in the catalog reminds readers why Mel was a treasure hunter. When asked, he always replied, "For the fun, romance, and adventure."

On the same page, Kim is shown as a tanned, vibrant man of 44, a son carrying on his father's tradition as President and CEO of the various Mel Fisher Family Enterprises. Kim personifies the impetus of the family legacy when he says, "The dream is not of treasure. Real treasure is the dream."

Throughout the catalog are many Fisher family photos that illustrate both the triumph and the tragedy that was required to recover the treasure artifacts. There are Mel and Deo wearing necklaces of Spanish gold chains; Mel and his youthful sons Kim and Kane displaying a bounty of gold chains on board a salvage boat; an at-sea portrait of the rusty M/V *Dauntless* with its "mailboxes" poised to be lowered into a calm sea; Mel with daughter Taffi on the M/V *JB Magruder*; Mel testifying in Federal Court; Mel in 1976, presenting the finest *Atocha* bronze cannon to Queen Sophia of Spain; and Dirk and Angel Fisher in the joyous days before the sinking of the M/V *Northwind,* among others that put the treasure items into their human perspective.

The catalog also presents brief stories of the *Atocha*, the *Santa Margarita* and the 1715 Spanish Plate Fleet in a two-page layout. The details set the stage for the historical importance that is inherent in every recovered artifact.

Six pages of the catalog are devoted to "treasure books of distinction and authenticity" that include *The Search for the Atocha* by historian Eugene Lyon; *Treasure of the Atocha* by R. Duncan Mathewson III, Archaeological Director of the search for the *Atocha; The Dreamweaver*, Mel's life story by Bob "Frogfoot" Weller; and *The Treasure Diver's Guide* by John S. Potter, Jr., a book that Mel considered essential in his orientation to treasure hunting, among others.

Another category in this section is "the magical lure of lost treasures of the sea" and included the titles *Shipwrecks of Florida* by Steven D. Singer; *New World Shipwrecks 1492-1825* by Robert and Jennifer Marx; *Treasure Hunt: The 16-year Search for the Lost Treasure Ship Atocha* by George Sullivan among others. Other book offerings were headlined "pirates—atlases—shipwrecks—buccaneers; Pirates Tales—Fact or fiction and Excitement;" and "Introducing Children to the Mystique of the Oceans." The children's book section included an *Atocha* coloring book by Katherine Amundson and Sandy McKinney that is very informative and historically accurate. The coloring books were autographed by Mel, himself, as the main character in the story.

For video collectors, the catalog offered a *National Geographic* video classic, *Quest for Treasure*, a 60-minute documentary film released in 1997 that told Mel's *Atocha* story in great detail. With footage taken over a number of the key years of discovery, this video contains exciting underwater sequences and extensive coverage of the treasure itself.

A&E The History Channel produced three 50-minute VHS documentaries featuring Mel that are also offered in the catalog. *The Search for the Treasure* documents the entire *Atocha* story based on the historic record. *The Search for the Queen's Jewels and the 1715 Plate Fleet* documents the sinking of eleven Spanish vessels during a hurricane along the Florida east coast. Over one thousand passengers and crewmembers lost their lives in these wrecks that were scattered across 200 miles of oceanfront. This film documents Mel's role in the recovery of treasures from these ships. The third A&E video is *City Confidential: Key West Pirates In Paradise*. This film features Mel as the King of the Conch Republic and celebrates Key West as the most charming pirate and shipwreck town in the world. The emotionality of both the successes and the losses of the treasure-hunting lifestyle are, however, fairly depicted.

An entire page in the catalog offers Mel Fisher memorial collectables. The first is a 36-page limited edition book by Bleth McHaley and Wendy Tucker that documents Mel's life leading up to the *Atocha* discovery and the stress on the Fisher family that followed. Titled *Mel Fisher World's Greatest Treasure Hunter*, the book contains a photo gallery from the Fisher family archives.

A second commemorative is the Mel Fisher Commemorative Medallion minted by the Franklin Mint in bronze from ancient copper ingots recovered from the *Atocha*. The 1-1/2 inch-diameter coin was sculpted by Don Everhart, a recognized artist in his field. The gift-boxed medallion is presented in a sealed acrylic display case with a removable stand. The display case allows both sides of the medallion to be shown. One side has a soft mat relief portrait of Mel with an inscription that reads, "The World's Greatest Treasure Hunter, Today's the Day!" Mel's signature also appears on the coin. The opposite side of the medallion has an artistic rendering of the *Atocha*. Each medallion was numbered and came with a Certificate of Authenticity. The list price for the medallion in its display case was $29.95. The medallion could also be purchased for $9.95 in a commemorative card. The coin in the card appears in a cutout window showing both front and back. The six-page card has The Search message on the "Today's the Day!" theme and a second spread— "The Discovery"—describing the excitement of the divers who discovered the treasure written by Pat Clyne.

Two final items on the commemorative page of the catalog were an 11 x 14" lithographed painting by Lewis Watkins, and a "motivational" 15" wide by 22" high poster. The composite-subject painting is titled "Atocha" and it depicts the great galleon in the Indies as she was in 1622 before the wreck. Mel is shown in relief as he appeared on the 1985 major discovery day. An underwater scene with divers on the shipwreck site completes the composition. Both painting lithograph and poster were listed at $9.95. The "Today's the Day" Mel Fisher poster features Mel's portrait above and a photo montage of golden treasures from the *Atocha* photographer Pat Clyne.

One of the most interesting aspects of whatever Mel Fisher Enterprises has done in the way of marketing itself is its highly professional attention to the details of projecting a quality image. Before there were websites to showcase a company in updated text, color photos, and promotional videos, there was a dependency on print goods like a catalog, a poster, or a brochure to connect to prospective buyers and expedition member supporters. Within the archives of the Fisher Enterprises companies, there is ample evidence that highly qualified copywriters, graphic designers, and photographers have been employed to create, through its history, images that elevate this company above its industry peers and moreover establishes its pre-eminence in offering the public participation in its exciting shipwreck adventures.

Treasure collectors know that gold shines forever. It does not tarnish like silver on the seabed. When it is a chain or a cup or bar pulled out of the bottom sand, the gold radiates its richness despite its nearly 400 years in the dark depths. The value of that gold artifact in 1622, however, is far, far different from what it is today. For its weight alone, the centuries have multiplied its value exponentially. Placed in its historic context like artifacts recovered from the *Atocha* and the *Santa Margarita*, the value soars higher each year, even in the 21st century.

The gold and silver and emerald artifacts offered in the 2000 Discover Day Treasures catalog provide a measurement of how real treasure escalates in value over a period of less than 15 years. In the year 2000, for example, an ounce of gold was valued at $279. Between 2011 and 2014 an ounce of gold sold for between $1,308 and $1,571 on the fluctuating world market.

The troy ounce price of silver since 2000 has depended on bullion demand for coinage and holdings for investment purposes. The value of museum-quality coins from the 17th century, however, has not been much affected by these price movements. As the 2000 catalog prices compared to today's retail prices prove, authentic silver coins recovered from the *Atocha* have done nothing but escalate over the years.

The *Atocha* transported hundreds of thousands of hand-stamped silver coins from mints in Potosi, Lima, and Mexico City. An eight-reales silver coin was generally equivalent to a month's pay for a sailor in the 1600s. Each piece-of-eight that was minted in the New World was uncirculated, and no two coins were exactly alike because of their methods of coinage. Newly poured silver was beaten into flat strips that were then cut into coin size planchets. The hand-engraved coin dies, front and back, were placed on the blank and struck with a hammer. The resulting struck coin was then weighed and any excess clipped off. This crude method produced uneven results to the extent that some coins of equal value in weight were often missing parts of the royal legend (translated) "Philip II By the Grace of God, King of Spain and the Indies."

One way of thinking about pieces-of-eight is to equate the eight-reale coin to the U.S. silver dollar, the four-reale coin to a fifty-cent piece, and the two-reale coin to the twenty-five cent piece or "quarter." During the circulation of the reales, there existed a practice of chiseling off small pieces from a coin's edge in order to accumulate value from these fragments. Perpetrators of this illegal act were termed "chiselers," and the term is used today to describe people who use unfair practices. The chiseling of the edges of gold and silver coins was eventually stopped by the minting of coins with a serrated or toothed edge.

On the best *Atocha* silver coins of eight, four, and two reales, the front or obverse side shows the Great Shield of Hapsburg with its representations for the various countries in Europe that were part of its alliance at that time. The reverse side is a hall-mark cross with two rampant lions and two castles (the Leon and Castile provinces of Spain), which indicates the alliance between the Catholic Church and the Spanish state.

A Grade One coin should exhibit a clean strike on both the obverse and reverse sides, and there should be no pitting or erosion evident except for details missing at the edges. A Grade Two should resemble a Grade One coin except it will have slight pitting caused by the corrosive effect of 400 years of salt water. A Grade Three coin shows pitting in excess of Grade Two. Many factors go into the condition of shipwreck-salvaged coins. Coins from some less skillful assayers may exhibit flat spots due to imperfect or worn dyes. A Grade Two silver coin can show one pristine side, where it faced another coin in the treasure chest, while the other side that was exposed is slightly pitted and corroded by the saltwater oxides. Grade Three coins that lay exposed outside of the chests have lost much of their detail. All coins recovered from the oceans, however, must undergo a period of reverse electrolysis to stabilize the coin, leach out the salt, and allow the incrustation to be picked away.

In 2000, a Grade One *Atocha* coin in the catalog listed for $2,055. A custom mount without chain was listed at an additional $1,075; $1,350; or $1,625 depending on the size of the coin. In 2014, a Grade One certified *Atocha* coin would bring at least $800 more than its 2000 quality equal.

Many gold escudo coins were recovered from the 1715 Spanish Treasure Fleet wreck sites. Far fewer escudos were recovered from the *Atocha,* who carried its gold mostly in the form of bars, disks, and chains. Most of the *Atocha* and *Santa Margarita* escudos were minted in Spain and were carried by wealthy Spanish passengers. There are fewer than 150 gold escudos in the *Atocha* collection because gold coins were not yet being minted in the New World of 1622; however, a sample set of gold coins that were found on the *Atocha* had been minted in Bogotá and were being shipped back to Spain for approval by the king.

The Seville gold coins were minted in eight, four, two, and one-escudo denominations. Eight-escudo coins are famously called "doubloons." Only one rare *Atocha* gold coin is offered in the catalog. It is a two-escudo coin of 6.7 grams in fine detail listed at $48,000. By contrast, an eight-escudo coin at 26.9 grams minted in Mexico from the 1715 Spanish Treasure Fleet is offered at $13,125, which included an 18K gold mount. A two-escudo 6.75-gram gold coin from the Santa Fe de Bogotá mint, also recovered from the 1715 Fleet, listed at $4,700.

Collectors of historic treasure artifacts do not need to be told that their collections escalate in value with each passing year; and as the possibilities diminish of recovering another *Atocha,* they also realize the historic importance of what they, through participation and preservation, have saved for cultural posterity. Of course, it has never been about the money, they will all attest. It is more about the excitement of holding empires in the palm of their hands and imagining how adventurers must have lived and died in a golden age of exploration.

20

The Bridge Between Eras

AFTER MEL FISHER DIED, it was obvious who had the best experiential and education credentials to head the multiple corporations of the Fisher family holdings. Kim had a university degree and two full years of a three-year law school curriculum. Anyone who would assume the CEO position of the Fisher family enterprises would do well to have that academic background. But Kim had also been an active treasure hunter in his pre-teen years and a dive master and salvage boat captain by the age of 17. He had earned that essential quality of leadership: respect among his peers and associates.

He was a man among men and women involved in a risky and sometimes dangerous trade. In addition, Kim had the steady temperament of leadership. He communicated calmness at the height of any storm, either at sea, in the corporate headquarters, and even when testifying in Federal Court. That's the kind of guy who you want at the helm of any challenging expedition. He will bring you through when others might fail.

Lee was the perfect companion for Kim in leading the Fisher companies into the 21st century. She not only had proven credentials as a treasure hunter herself, but she also had the executive organizational experiences that are necessary in the management of a company as diverse as the Fisher family enterprises. Lee was also tough minded enough to weather the storms of the couple's chosen lifestyle. She could be very stalwart against adversarial tides that rocked the corporate boat. She possessed strengths that were different from those displayed by Kim, but when combined with his, made them a formidable leadership couple. Alone, however, they could not reach the goals that their company had to achieve each year. They needed the dedication, skills, and talents of other individuals who were vital to the successful continuation of the company.

Photo by Mel Fisher's Treasures

Jan Stauch is the corporate finance manager.

Lee cites two key individuals who bridged the continuation of the company from Mel's leadership to Kim's. Jan Stauch, the corporate finance manager, has juggled the economic cycles and the tax responsibilities for the many companies under the Fisher family enterprises umbrella since 1989. When times were slim in the income area, she found the resources to keep the salvage boats in fuel and crew supplies so that they could keep on searching. Even when Mel did not know his bank balance, Jan knew the company's liquid capital position and could account for every dollar coming and going. Jan was the keeper of all financial secrets. It was a huge responsibility, and Kim and Lee say that without Jan's dedication and skill, there were times when the corporate ship might have sunk without her heroic efforts.

Jan moves through the corporate offices with determined efficiency. Her facial expression is often that of a person involved in a complex mathematical calculation. Do not block her way when she is en route to Kim or Lee's office. She is on a mission. But meet Jan at the coffee machine, and she has a ready smile. Her lack of chit-chat she attributes to her shyness. She is reluctant to tell stories about herself. For movie casting, Jan would play the attractive blonde-streaked brunette CPA who has to break the news to Tom Hanks that he is being audited by the IRS. She would display empathy, but she would be necessarily firm with him in explaining the realities. Tom Hanks would slide lower and lower in his chair, and the scene with Jan would win him another Academy Award.

Gary Randolph is another continuity bridge from the old to the new leadership era. He was hired by founder Mel Fisher as a diver, but within eleven months, Gary became the captain of the 90-foot salvage vessel *JB Magruder* in December 1995. On his first trip as captain, his crew recovered a gold coin and a gold chain, which was the first of the many treasure finds under his leadership. By 1997 his salvage skills and dedication earned him the position of Operations Manager. Today Gary is Vice President and Director of Operations, where he works in a close collaboration with Kim, the next generation of Fisher-led treasure hunting.

In spanning 20 years of company history, Gary has manifested the core enthusiasm and personal determination that it takes to be a professional salvor. As the Vice President for Operations, Gary oversees the day to day activity of half a dozen seagoing vessels, their captains, and their crews. He also manages maintenance, re-supply, advanced technology, and the planning of each treasure expedition. The range of his activity is not restricted to the Florida Keys. The company contracts with additional salvage vessels and crews to explore additional shipwreck sites. It is the search that ultimately motivates Kim and Gary as it did Mel. The day after the *Atocha* Mother Lode was found, Mel was already talking about another treasure ship to be sought. The adventure is always in the search. The recovery of great wealth is an end game, wonderful in its accomplishment, but only momentarily satisfying for the true explorer. What is next? That's the question.

For Gary, there is also another question. How do we search better, more efficiently? What do we have to do to be the leaders in other seas and oceans? The persistent search for the *Atocha* sterncastle is thus just one of their salvage targets. Like Mel

Gary Randolph is the V.P. of operations.

Fisher, the company leadership is always researching the location of other shipwrecks as they simultaneously develop innovations in underwater search technology. In 2014, a breakthrough search vehicle named *Dolores* was in the water close on the coordinates of the next major treasure find: a ship called *The Lost Merchant*.

When Lee married Kim in 1989 and joined the treasure hunting team, she was an experienced diver and proven adventurer. For her first ten years with the company, Mel was in the leadership chair, and everything revolved around his ventures that were both far and wide. Lee and Kim, like everyone else, might be surprised by where he would send them next. The internal management of the company was not Kim or Lee's concern.

When Scott was born in 1997, Lee became a stay-at-home mom. Then Ricky arrived in 1999, and her focus was entirely on home and family. Kim had actually assumed the company CEO responsibilities in 1998 when Mel's health deteriorated due to cancer. With his father's death in December 1998, Kim was handed a tangled web of companies, ventures, and contracts that Mel had initiated. For the first time, Kim saw the true, bare-bones financial condition of the Fishers' myriad holdings as well as their financial obligations. Then, too, there was also the management of ongoing court cases that required Kim's attention.

21

Travels with the Children

IN THE EARLY 2000S, WITH Kim's three older sons by a previous marriage—Jeremy, Sean, and Neko—either grown or in college, Kim and Lee decided to include their young sons Scott and Rick in all their travels. Most of their trips were made for scouting treasure sites and lasted only two to three weeks, but there were opportunities for much longer stays in the Bahamas and the Turks and Caicos islands where they were only an hour's flight time from Key West. With Kim as CEO, the structure of the company allowed them to provide executive management via telephone and weekly Skype meetings.

One of their earliest travel adventures with Scott and Rick, then aged three and two, was to the French Commonwealth of Dominica, the most pristine wilderness island in the Caribbean, with lush mountainous rainforests; rare plant, animal, and bird species; and over 300 rivers and streams. The island was named by Christopher Columbus in 1493 for the day of the week that it was sighted; Sunday is "Domingo" in Latin. Formed

The Fishers visit Disneyland

by geothermic-volcanic activity, it is the youngest island in the Lesser Antilles and was colonized during its history by Spain, France, and Great Britain.

The eco-knowledgeable tour guides were fascinating indigenous black people who traced their ancestry to the Island Caribs or Kalinago people. In the warm coastline waters, there were coral reefs for snorkeling, and in deeper water, sperm whales and dolphins to be seen year round.

The volcanic nature of the island caused the inshore ocean waters to bubble like champagne. While diving, the Fishers experienced the bubbles as a warmth that enveloped them. Another educational oddity was the profusion of road signs on the island. To serve the fluctuations in colonial rule, the signs were tri-lingual in French, Spanish, and English.

Lee remembers a family canoe trip down a Dominica river that felt like they were going back in time. Every bend in the tropical forest river promised beauty and adventures. When the canoes landed on the banks of a remote village where the adults were dressed in sarongs, and their children were mostly naked, it was fun to watch their boys interact with the locals. It did not take long for all the children to overcome the language barrier and begin to play.

When the boys were six and five, there was a memorable trip to Roatan, the largest of Honduras's Bay Islands, where they played with monkeys and fed bananas to huge iguanas that were nearly their own size.

When the boys were nine and eight, there was an extensive stay in the Bahamas that lasted nearly a year. To help home-school the boys (who were third and fourth graders by then), Lee invited Lynn Redding, wife of company engineer Shawn Redding, and their two sons Parker and Sawyer to join them on Grand Bahama Island.

That year in the Bahamas, the two boys experienced their first open-water dive. With Lee close at hand, the boys descended to a sunken ship to view its exposed 86 cannons. Later the same day, while walking on the beach, they came upon a lobster over

Photo by Lee Wiegand

The boys Scott and Rick show off their first lost teeth.

two feet long. Lee questions which discovery gave the young boys a bigger thrill. With so much world travel and adventure already accumulated by the boys, there was evidence that their threshold for excitement was getting higher.

Lee remembers one day while they were back in Key West for business. Kim had brought home a solid gold bar recovered from a treasure ship to impress the boys, but after a brief acknowledgment, all they wanted to know was what was for dinner. At another time, Kim was on a deep-water project, and he was live streaming a view of the most famous sunken ship in history—the Titanic. Lee called the boys to the computer to witness the amazing real-time video stream of the Titanic's bow, but the boys soon went back to their video games.

"We did get their full attention, however, on a business trip to New York City," Lee recalls. "A friend offered his Learjet for the trip, and he had a private limo waiting for us on arrival. The driver was instructed to take us anywhere we wanted to go for the weekend. We dropped off our luggage at the Waldorf-Astoria and then went straight to FAO Schwartz, the legendary toy company where kids are greeted at the door by men dressed as toy soldiers. The Fifth Avenue store is rightly called the quintessential children's wonderland. Scott and Rick were thrilled."

After a year in the Bahamas, the family relocated their home base to the Turks and Caicos, islands north of Hispaniola and 647 miles east-southeast from Miami. The eight main islands and its 299 smaller islands were then a British Overseas Territory. The environment was another tropical paradise of low, flat limestone islands with extensive marshes and mangrove swamps. The climate is relatively dry; and with limited freshwater resources, homeowners divert the rainwater off their roofs into private cisterns for drinking and bathing. The bounty of the

Lucayan Archipelago provides a feast of spiny lobster, conch, and other shellfish.

Here Lee accepted the responsibility to homeschool the boys. School lessons lasted from 9 a.m. till noon. After a quick lunch, they would get into the car and begin to explore the island, visiting the many villages and tasting the different foods. Many days they would stop to swim and pass the hours there till suppertime. One day to her amazement, the boys announced (with their British accents), "Mummy, we want to go home to our mates."

Young Scott and Rick visit the Arenal
volcano in Costa Rica with their parents.

They were adamant. Kim and Lee had always agreed they would travel as long as the boys were happy, too. A decision was made. It was time to go home to Key West where they arrived just in time for the birth of their grandson Max. As Scott and Rick reunited with their friends in Key West, the days were filled with learning to scuba, spearfish, catch lobster, and how to run a boat—a typical Key West childhood.

The travel adventures of Scott and Rick did not end in the Turks and Caicos, however. In Costa Rica, they witnessed an active lava flow, zip-lined over an 1800-foot crevasse, learned to ride horseback, and to also milk a cow. On a trip to Europe, the boys saw the historic sights of London, and then they had a hiking adventure into the mountains of Bulgaria.

On the Yucatán Peninsula in Mexico, west of Cancun, the boys visited the soaring pyramids and massive temples of the ancient Mayans, Chichen Itza. The settlement is one of the grandest archaeological sites in the world. In the local markets, Lee remembers the boys learning to barter. It was a useful skill when they visited Jamaica. With Key West as their homeport, and high school friends being a priority, Kim and Lee are grateful for the wonderful memories they have to treasure.

22

An Amazing Energy Couple

THEY ARE UP EARLY in the morning to coordinate the coming day that includes two teenaged sons at home, a wide-ranging and complex business operation, and the social and charitable connections that they have built up over the years. Then, in addition, there always seems to be a houseguest or two to also be considered.

Kim keeps regular office hours and rides a 14-speed custom bicycle the five miles to the Greene Street office every day. His daily attire is a company short-sleeve shirt, shorts, and sandals. Especially when there are salvage boats searching for treasure at sea, or a highly technical piece of equipment being tested, he can be updated on the cellphone that he always carries. Kim's bike comes with him on the elevator to the fourth floor and will be rolled into his office.

Kim is greeted on arrival by his Administrative Director Joe Sweeney, a former combat decorated U.S. Navy Chief who served three tours in Iraq, one while on loan to the Army. Even on the weekends, Joe knows how to find Kim and to alert him to any developments that require his attention. Joe is a proud native of the New Jersey shore where as a teenager, he once collected the $2 cover charge for a lounge show by Bruce Springsteen. Joe has attitude that requires everyone to stay straight with him, but his good humor and dazzling efficiency make them enjoy it. Off hours, Joe is the most popular shipmate at the Galleon Resort Marina where the owners of multimillion-dollar yachts invite Joe to go fishing every weekend.

Coincidentally, the Galleon Resort was named after the replica Spanish galleon that Mel Fisher had constructed to serve as his Key West museum and office space. Called the *Golden Doubloon* and promoted as a tourist attraction, the big wooden boat was moored to the dock at the end of Front Street. The *Golden Doubloon* was the place where the media had rushed to view great treasure finds. It was also the site of Dirk and Angel Fisher's wedding with over a hundred celebrants overflowing the decks

Administrative Director Joe Sweeney is Kim's key man in the office.

of the galleon onto the docks. Then in July 1975, it became the focus of the intense grief and mourning of their tragic deaths.

The *Golden Doubloon*, with its rotting hull and many leaks, was kept afloat by 14 sump pumps, until they were overwhelmed in 1982, and the boat sunk alongside the dock.

At the office Joe protects Kim from the "small stuff" that would interrupt the CEO's focus on the major operational decisions of the company. If you saw them working together—Joe at his outside communications console and Kim in his adjacent executive office—you might believe that you were seeing partners at work instead of a boss and his key man.

Lee has Mom duties before she can leave for the office. The boys must pass her inspection, get their lunch money on school days, and otherwise brief her on their plans for the day. Lee has always been a company officer since Kim became its CEO in 1999, but she also played a support role by hosting Division Week expedition members, and by responding to situational needs. Then in January 2014, Lee moved into the Executive Vice-President's office next to Kim's to direct the re-organization of the Retail and Investor Relations departments. This move required her to schedule a full-time workweek at the office.

Most days, Lee drives to their building, parks across the street in a parking garage, and unlocks the executive office by 8:20 a.m. just a few minutes before Joe arrives. Joe, carrying his *New York Post*, his favorite cup of coffee, and a Cuban bread breakfast sandwich, is non-plussed when Lee beats him into the office because Lee starts fast and already knows the objectives of her workday. Lee has begun directing staff activities by the time Kim arrives around nine.

The first order of the business day for Kim may be a briefing by Joe on the overnight status of their immediate concerns.

Joe, who has over 15 years as a paralegal for the Judge Advocate General (JAG) Corps, is well versed to brief Kim on the several active court cases that affect the company. Joe has his "special" contacts in the Federal and state courts that keep him up to date on filed motions and upcoming decisions. What has been termed "the trouble with treasure" usually involves court cases to establish salvage rights.

Another primary topic to begin Kim's day would be the current status of all vessels in the Fisher salvage fleet. When at sea with electronic search devices and divers in the water to explore the bottom, "Today's the day" founder Mel Fisher's constant adage, might be announced at any hour. Gary Randolph, Vice President of Operations, would probably be the first to notify Kim of a new treasure find, but the executive office always monitors its ships at sea.

In the spring of 2014, after years of development at great expense, a group of advanced-level technicians under the direction of Gary Randolph were conducting sea trials of a device that should revolutionize the treasure salvaging industry. *Dolores*, named after Kim's mother, is beyond state-of-the-art technology. It is the future. Its very complex technology is both proprietary and very secret. *Dolores* was the major topic of interest at all levels of the corporate structure. She was the darling of all their economic futures.

That spring and summer, Lee's focus was setting retail sales goals and motivating her associates to exceed them. *Atocha* treasure artifacts do not become available capital until they are sold. The retail side of the operation with three locations provides the cash resources to bridge the gap between one significant treasure find and the next one. With expenses for staff, crews, multiple boats and ships, *Dolores* development, and court costs running

*Lee and Kim are expert spear fishermen who catch the
limit every season to share with friends and family.*

into millions of dollars annually, Lee's retail outlets are the cash
cows that underwrite everything else. And under her supervision and vision, by May, that division of the company was already
exceeding its sales goals.

Investor Relations is a sales and service operation managed
by Shawn Cowles, a long-term associate of the company. It has
goals, too—$3.6 million worth of goals. That's what it takes to
finance a single year of treasure explorations. What is being sold
is not yet material. It is not even a promise of return. It is an
intangible wrapped up in the romantic ideal of adventure. Yes,
you can dive on the *Atocha* wreck site. Yes, you can sift in sluice
trays for *Atocha* emeralds. You may be rewarded greatly, but the
primary opportunity that is being presented is the participation
itself in something that is adventurous and fun and historically
huge in significance.

In reviewing the positioning of the Investor Relations office,
Lee wanted it more visible and inviting to customers shopping

in the Museum building Greene Street retail store. Since *Atocha* coins were being sold for thousands of dollars each, and *Atocha* emeralds for tens of thousands of dollars each, customers making those purchases pre-qualified themselves for expedition membership. For those, and anyone else who expressed interest, Shawn and his two associates invited the individuals to not only view a four to six-minute video about the membership experience but to also be photographed with *Atocha* gold chains and gold bars in front of a Mel Fisher's Treasures backdrop. The photographs could be taken with the visitor's camera or by the Investor Relations staff and sent to them as an e-mail attachment. Lee measured success by how many people during the week viewed the video, asked about membership costs, and then had their photographs taken with the *Atocha* gold. There was, of course, a follow-up system put in place to determine if the visitors had continuing interest after leaving Key West. There was no barrier, obviously, if the person wanted to move into Shawn's private office and make a deal the same day.

Primary in the Investor Relations division is the renewal of annual memberships. Shawn has an impressive record of renewals at a 70% rate, but that means that 30% have to be added to the new-member roster.

Lee's business day addresses the management needs of both divisions. Often she meets with daughter-in-law Star Fisher who is the retail sales supervisor and the Inventory Manager. Star brings her Great Dane Bucci—named for a shot of strong Cuban espresso—to work, and he is a quiet but massive presence in her office. *Atocha* coins, for example, have to be matched with their certification documents for sale or purchase. It is not uncommon for a surviving family relative of an early expedition member to offer *Atocha, Santa Margarita*, or even 1715 shipwreck coins distributed or sold in the 1970s and 1980s. Sandy in Curating must verify the coins from original documents and appraise them for current retail value. Only then can the company make a purchase offer for resale in the retail shops.

Over the years they have encountered both fakes and frauds and even counterfeit Certificates of Authenticity. Their intention is to be both considerate and fair with the sellers. Some who claim to just have discovered the treasure coins in a family safe-deposit box, however, have no certificates with its photos back-and-front of the coins, and no identification number that matches the Fisher company's artifact database. No offer can be made on these uncertified coins.

At 5 p.m., unless there are important matters pending, Kim rolls his bike out of his office and takes the waterside bike trail route home. Lee promises to wrap up her day and lay aside the project folders on her desk and follow soon. Some days, she has a roast or ham slow cooking in a large crockpot, and the family will eat at home. But often they will go out to a favorite restaurant. Every Wednesday night at 8 p.m. they go to Manga Manga, an Italian pasta restaurant where they know the owners Heather and Mike.

Kim and Lee are back home by 9:30 p.m. There is time for the boys, and then early to bed. Kim and Lee watch no television. They read no newspapers. Their meals at home or out in a restaurant are nutrition based as reflects Lee's holistic orientation. They take only homeopathic medications. They are as grounded and focused on the successful continuation of the treasure salvaging enterprise as two married partners can be. Kim and Lee take care of their bodies for endurance sake by biking and taking to the water as tandem diving spear fishermen. They know the best spots, both in the backcountry and out on the reefs, where they catch the limits of lobster, hogfish, snapper, or grouper to share with family and friends. Kim also has a personal trainer for regular workouts in a gym, and Lee attends Bikram yoga classes three times a week.

Kim and Lee like to have fun. Lee's laugh can be exuberant while Kim's is more understated but unrestrained. They are welcome companions for a party, a boat ride, or a walk down Duval Street where the sidewalks are full of tourists and Key West's nighttime entertainers. In mid-July Kim and Lee host Mel Fisher Days, an annual celebration to honor the anniversary of Mel and Deo's discovery of the *Atocha* Mother Lode. The Thursday-through-Sunday schedule of public events includes a Street Fair and a treasure hunt, where the grand prize of $5,000 is paid with a chest of silver dollars. One hundred percent of all net proceeds from Mel Fisher Days events are donated to Wesley House Family Services that provides services to children and families throughout the Florida Keys. 2014 celebrated the 28th anniversary of Mel Fisher Days

In mid-October Kim and Lee usually demonstrate the fun-ride of being a Key Wester by joining the revelers on Duval Street for the 10-day party now known worldwide as Fantasy Fest. The annual adult-themed extravaganza was started in 1979 by a small group of Key West locals as a visitor attraction during a usually off-season month. It has grown every year since to become a major Key West attraction that fills the city with tens of thousands of costumed fun-seekers from around the world. When the population swells overnight from 25,000 to include 75,000 tourists, the residents joke that "the island sinks one foot that day." To picture Fantasy Fest, think New Orleans Mardi Gras and Rio de Janeiro's Carnival with body painting optional. Think "spectacle."

The 2014 theme of Fantasy Fest was Animeted Dreams and Adventures. Anime is a traditional Japanese form of animation that sparked a costuming lifestyle known as "cosplay." For Key West costume lovers, it was East Meets West in a fantasy collision of style and creativity. You had to see it to believe it. All was on display at the Captain Morgan Parade and any night of the Fest along the mile-long Duval Street where a Street Fair was also staged with arts, crafts, and food and beverage vendors. Many houses and businesses in the party area competed for the Reddy Ice Fantasy Façade Awards by decorating according to the Fest theme. Award categories included Private Residence, Guest House, Small Business and Big Business, and even Honorable Mentions were coveted as establishments went all out in their passions to wildly decorate.

On less extravagant days than Fantasy Fest, Kim and Lee provide boat rides for houseguests, friends, and family who visit. These are usually four-hour trips around the entire shoreline of Key West, with a stop along the way to swim off a sand bar and explore a small mangrove key. Lee serves as the back-country tour guide for these outings while Kim, so at home at the wheel of a fast sport-fishing boat that doubles for runs out to the salvage vessels, navigates through the tricky channels and sand bars that challenge boaters in the shallow depths of these waters. Kim likes to run hard and fast in open water. With the wind in his face and a smile on his lips, you see a contented man in his natural element.

23

The Quiet Man

KIM FISHER IS TALL (6 ft. 5 inches) and lanky in an athletic way. He rides a bike about five miles each way across Key West to his Mel Fisher's Treasures office in the Mel Fisher Maritime Heritage Museum building on 200 Greene Street. The Museum is located at the heart of tourist activity in Key West. The giant cruise ships dock across the street and can be viewed as skyscrapers between the Hyatt Sunset Harbor Hotel and the Westin Resort Hotel. Within an easy walking distance is the Ernest Hemingway House and the bar watering holes that he made famous. President Harry Truman came for eleven vacations to the "Little White House" on Truman Annex, and surrounding all is the Caribbean architectural ambience of Old Town Key West. People born on Key West are called Conchs. Kim is what is termed a fresh-water Conch. He has been a resident of the island for only 43 years.

If you are a fan of classic films, you might want to compare Kim Fisher in appearance and attitude to the slow talking, strong, silent types that actor Gary Cooper portrayed as he moves through his sometimes frenetic and dangerous occupation as the President and CEO of the various Mel Fisher family enterprises. See Cooper in the award-winning movie adapted from the Hemingway novel *For Whom the Bell Tolls*, with Ingrid Bergman.

Kim earned his father's legacy of being the foremost undersea treasure hunter in modern history by over 50 years of on-the-job experience. He learned to snorkel and then to dive with scuba gear before he was a teenager; and by the age of 17, he was given the command of a dive vessel—a converted tugboat, the *Southwind*. His captaincy, which included himself diving on the treasure search sites, came at a time of intense activity as his father and brothers worked the waters off Key West for the elusive legendary treasure galleons *Nuestra Señora de Atocha* and *Santa Margarita* which sunk during a hurricane in 1622.

During those years before 1973, when the first evidence of the *Atocha* was verified, the Fisher family had risked everything on their quest. Failure was not an option in the atmosphere of Mel Fisher's unbridled enthusiasm and confidence; but if the Mother Lode of the *Atocha*'s treasure was not found, the Fishers stood to lose all their property and assets as well as their reputations. This challenging environment of make-it-or-break-it was the family and social world that Kim experienced from childhood to his adult years.

If you work around Kim Fisher today, one of the first impressions will be his seemingly constant state of calmness. He is always engaging with an easy smile, but there is no excess in his manner or in his conversations. Kim deals with constant trouble within the treasure salvage industry, as we will learn. If it is not the government changing the rules of admiralty law governing shipwrecks, competitors muddying the waters of industry credibility, or outright fraudulent operators who sell fakes attributed to his treasure rights, it is a United Nations agency or a foreign government seeking to stop or control any salvage operations of historic shipwrecks.

All these challenges to future Fisher salvage ventures must be met head on by legal actions that last for years and run up attorney costs in the millions of dollars. What great effort of treasure hunting does it take to satisfy a legal bill of $1 million? What kind of toll regarding psychological stress does it cost? Whatever it is, you will not get a quick reading by Kim's behavior in his executive offices. Associates agree that Kim Fisher is maybe the calmest man under fire that they have ever known. Some of them are veterans of combat in Vietnam, Iraq, or Afghanistan, and they would choose Kim to be their leader in the most dangerous circumstances because he is so character strong and so unshakable.

So what does this action-adventure commodore of a treasure salvage fleet do after he has talked to his captains at sea? He rides his high-tech bicycle along the Key West beachfront and goes home to relax with a book in his Lazyboy chair where he can stretch out barefooted with his Kindle propped up on two pillows. Then he reads until a nap overcomes him just before the call to supper. You'd like to imagine super cool Hollywood actor Gary Cooper doing much the same thing when he returned home from fantasy adventures. The difference, of course, is that Kim Fisher has a real world of serious challenges to face every day where his rock-steady calmness cannot be an act.

24

The Other Lee Fisher

EVERY WEDNESDAY IN A year of Wednesdays, Lee Fisher leaves the executive responsibilities at her office at noon, finds a quick lunch en route, and drives the length of Key West to the next Key, Stock Island. Kim and company associates know where she is going, but they do not know what she will do there. If they followed her and observed, they would learn another side of Lee.

Lee's Wednesday destination is the Star of the Sea Outreach Mission food bank. The vital service to supplement the diets of disadvantaged individuals and families was begun in 2006 by St. Mary's Star of the Sea Catholic Church, and it is now one of the largest food banks in South Florida, serving as many as 4,000 people a month. A small staff supported by devoted volunteers process a monthly average of 50,000 pounds of food by buying $5,000 of food at discount and by making daily trips to grocery stores, restaurants, businesses, relief agencies, and private donors to essentially rescue food before it can be discarded. The labor-intensive process is deemed "food recovery." The USDA estimates that 30% to 40% of all food produced in the U.S. goes to waste.

The labor to unload trucks, sort, store, refrigerate, and stock the shelves of the donated food is as demanding as any medium-sized chain supermarket, but it must, for budget sake, be done by volunteers. Every act of food bank management and labor, however, comes down to the objective of the service—the indigent individuals who present themselves in desperate need. Monday through Friday between 10 a.m. and 5 p.m. they come, some with their babies and young children, as many as 200 a day.

They arrive to be validated for need as the most vulnerable human beings that one could ever meet. But more than the food, the free clothing, toiletries, diapers, pet food, and other household basics, what neighbors want in these circumstances is a non-judgmental compassion that preserves their dignity. The individuals who engage in these face-to-face encounters and accompany the clients of the food bank through its aisles are called "walkers." Lee Fisher is one of the most dependable volunteer walkers at Star of the Sea. The service requires a unique gentility that is humility based, and it is not the role at the food bank that many people want to undertake. In many ways, unloading the trucks is the preferred choice.

In Lee's 1:30 to 5 p.m. walker shift, she will meet, greet, and guide as many as 40 men and women representing a wide cross-section of age and ethnicity. Often she greets a limited-English speaker in their home Spanish language. Over the months, Lee has learned the Spanish words for many items on the food bank shelves. A pre-screened client presents Lee with a small rectangular slip of paper that reads "emergency" (the client has no refrigeration or stove to prepare food), "individual," or "family" with a number to indicate how many must be fed. The client is allowed one visit per week because the food is meant to be supplemental rather than a total resource. The demand mandates this policy.

Lee walks backwards directing the individual to select items along an established path. A gentle discipline is required to make sure that resources are conserved for the 1000 or more people who depend on the food bank every week. Stopping before shelves of canned vegetables, a client may choose one. At shelves of bagged rice and black beans, one of each may be taken. At the fresh-vegetable area, many items are available. In the bread section, a family representative may select two. There are even tempting dessert shelves of pies, pastries, and cookies near their expiration dates that have been donated. MRE's (meals ready to eat that cook within their own packaging) are reserved for "emergency" category clients. At the end of the walk through the aisles, the clients have plastic bags full of nourishing foods. Often at the exit door, eye contact is made, and a mutual blessing is exchanged between the volunteer walker and the individual served.

Lee always introduces herself and learns and uses the name of the individuals whom she escorts. After a year of Wednesdays, Lee and many visitors to the food bank recognize each other, and the greeting for the clients is one of happy relief. They feel comfortable with Lee, and that in itself is one of her gifts.

At the Mel Fisher's Treasures headquarters, Lee is a demanding executive who led the 2014 reorganization of their retail operations. One could recognize Lee as managing by objectives and requiring mutually agreed goals to be met. To witness the softer side of Lee at the Star of the Sea food bank might thus be a revelation to her business associates and employees. Any Wednesday, they could shadow her and see a remarkable degree of selflessness and gentle compassion worthy of both surprise and admiration. And if you ask Lee why she was such a faithful volunteer in the challenging environment of poverty and need, she has replied, "I love the people there. Everyone is open. There are no façades, just genuine caring for each other."

Lee has another special interest that might surprise people. She introduces the subject this way.

"Through the years, my love of learning has drawn me to continue my studies with many great teachers at numerous institutes. My favorite, of course, has been The Monroe Institute."

The mission statement of the internationally known non-profit charitable organization is clear:

"The Monroe Institute (TMI) furthers the experience and exploration of consciousness, expanded awareness, and discovery of self through technology, education, research, and development."

TMI was founded by Robert Monroe who was a pioneer and visionary in the study of human consciousness. His investigations employed a scientific means based on an audio technology that he engineered. Active for over 30 years, the institute is located in the Blue Ridge Mountains near Faber, Virginia. Tens of thousands of people have attended the institute's residential and outreach programs. Lee attended courses at the institute for a decade before she was invited to join its board of directors.

About her board service, Lee says, "My passion is research, and now I have been given the opportunity to work with the greatest minds from around the world, sharing their wisdom and dreams in a united effort to raise the awareness of human consciousness."

As prestigious as her position on The Monroe Institute may be, it is also demanding, and Lee has made the long trip from Key West to the Charlottesville, Virginia airport many times, and then taken a car for an hour's drive into the mountains. One aspect of the board is to facilitate ongoing research projects into the evolution of human consciousness and to then provide experiential education programs as an extension of Robert Monroe's legacy.

Robert Monroe was dedicated to provide something of value to humanity that would help people, regardless of race, color, creed, or national or ethnic origin, to lead better and more fulfilling lives. Lee Fisher has made a commitment to The Monroe Institute to serve its goal of expanding human consciousness. That, one must admit, is a very serious undertaking.

Kim in the Classroom

KIM HAS OFTEN BEEN invited to appear in classrooms to talk about the historic adventure of treasure hunting. He may out-fit a student in dive gear and have other visual aids to keep the children's interest. They, of course, all want to hear about sharks.

Most sharks, Kim tells them, want nothing to do with humans. There may be danger if there are bloody fish in the water, but mostly sharks go their own way. Even the large bar-racuda with their sharp display of teeth are more curious about divers than threatening. Since barracuda have eyes set on the side of their heads, they do not see well, and so they have to come close to see what a diver is doing. The fact that they open and close their mouths to breathe appears like they are preparing to bite; but even when surrounded by a school of five-foot-long barracuda, experienced divers are not worried.

If they seem disappointed by the truth about sharks and barracuda, the children become excited when the gold bars and silver pieces-of-eight are passed around. The gold does not lose its color and luster from over 300 years under the sea, they are told. When a diver sees a glimmer of gold, he may be able to pull a long chain of gold out of the sand. Silver bars and coins, however, become encrusted by seawater. Kim shows the children both encrusted silver coins as well as those that have been conserved and restored.

After the story telling and the hands-on experience with the treasure itself, Kim invites questions. Some child always asks, "How do you get started treasure hunting?"

Kim has a ready and practical reply. "You get started in the library."

The reference is, of course, to Eugene Lyon's groundbreaking discoveries in Spain's great library Archive of the Indies in Seville. Lyon's scholarship and his ability to read the old Castilian Spanish language script of ship manifests and salvage reports was key to locating both the *Atocha* and the *Santa Margarita*. Kim was not kidding when he pointed the school children to the library.

Thinking about Dr. Lyon, Kim acknowledged the key role that he played in the successful search for the *Atocha*.

"Dr. Lyon was a close friend of my mother and father; and one day while he was researching for his Ph.D. in the Spanish archives in Seville, he discovered the original manifest of the *Atocha*. As he deciphered it, he realized that the Spanish in 1622 called all the Florida Keys the "Matecumbes." Dad at that time was living on Matecumbe Key and searching for the *Atocha* there. Gene told Dad that he had also found the salvage reports naming the Marquesa Key as the actual site of Spanish efforts to salvage the 1622 fleet shipwrecks. This location was a hundred miles west of where Dad was searching. The Marquesa Keys had been named to honor the expedition leader of the salvage efforts. The news prompted Dad to move our entire family, boats, and crews to Key West.

"The Marquesa Key is very unique. It was formed by a meteorite striking so hard that it pushed up the sand that created the key's formation."

The usual formation of a "caye" that becomes identified as a "key" in Florida and a "cay" in the Bahamas is for sand and dirt sediments to be driven by currents and storms onto a coral reef. The build-up around the reef then breaks the water surface and builds into a caye. Sea birds, who are very instrumental in building cayes, then drop seeds that are fertilized by their guano bird manure. This accounts for the vegetation that appears on the island cayes. The most important vegetation, however, for the Florida Keys is the growth of the red mangroves. The tangled masses of their roots capture the tidal sands and thus build the familiar low-elevation islands. Another defining characteristic of cayes is that they do not have a natural freshwater source.

By contrast, the land masses surrounded by water that qualify geologically as islands are either formed by volcanic action like Hawaii, Japan, and the Philippines, or result from shifts of a continental plate that "float" them on top of the earth's mantle. Greenland and Australia are examples of continental islands.

The geological life of a caye is tenuous. Small ones arise and disappear on a timetable measured in hurricanes. Inhabited cayes, however, like Key West, can have both strategic and economic importance that must be defended. In 1980, the Florida Keys were inundated by thousands of refugees who were granted a small time window of escape from Cuba by their dictator Fidel Castro. The evacuees were assembled in the Mariel harbor, and their migration to Florida was thus termed the "Mariel Boatlift." Unknown then, Castro emptied his prisons of criminals and included them among the boatlift crowds. For the U.S. Coast Guard and the Emigration Bureau, the problems of handling the arrival of the desperate illegal aliens were enormous. The repercussions of the Mariel Boatlift lasted for years; and for a period in 1980, the U.S. Border Patrol erected a series of roadblocks on the bridge from the Florida Keys to search vehicles returning to the mainland for illegal immigrants. The economic effect of the roadblocks on Florida Keys tourism was disastrous.

When Key West was unable to negotiate relief from the Border Patrol roadblocks, Mayor Dennis Wardlow declared Key West independent of the United States and renamed it the Conch Republic. The secession of April 23, 1982 did not last long, but it did establish that the citizens of even a small cay (or key) can muster a great deal of pride in their unique identity.

26

The Untold Stories

THE NOTION THAT MEL Fisher's Treasures and its other affili-
ated companies is a family operation extends not only to blood-
related Fishers but also to everyone who is associated with them.
The personal stories of how these individuals support each other
has no hierarchal scale. It is top down and bottom up. The acts
of sincere kindness and quiet compassion are never made public.
Even within the company, the privacy between giver and receiver
is respected. In any meaningful documentation of what Kim and
Lee bring to their company, however, a few of these stories need
to be told.

Alfredo Aguero, who works security for the Greene Street
retail jewelry store, had a serious dilemma involving a family crisis. His mother had Alzheimer's disease and required constant
care, and his father was becoming too infirm to continue his role
in her care. It fell to Alfredo to arrange for their welfare, but in
the process, his father died. The toll of Alfredo's responsibility
required him to be away from his job for two full months.

Key West is an expensive town to live in as a resident. Working-class people often have to have two jobs to meet the high rent and living expenses. Two months out of work for anyone would threaten their ability to stay on the island. That threat did not complicate Alfredo's service to his disabled parents because Kim and Lee kept paying him his salary the entire duration of his crisis.

Alfredo Aguero at his security post.

Most work days, Alfredo is at his place by the entry door to the company jewelry store where both Kim, with his bicycle, and Lee enter and leave the building. Alfredo also controls access to the elevator that takes Kim and Lee to their fourth-floor offices, and he handles the two heavy metal doors of the antique freight conveyance as part of his service. Greetings are always exchanged, and a casual observer might be impressed by the politeness of their encounter. The depth of their relationship, however, would be missed.

Alfredo Aguero in 2014 had been part of the Fisher company family for fourteen years. Lee is conscious that he never forgets to remember her birthday.

On the Monday after Division Week in 2014, Alfredo escorted Lee to the elevator, and in a private moment, he returned to her his paycheck for working security at the Saturday night gala expedition members' party at the Casa Marina resort. He whispered to her that his service to her and Kim at the party was a gift. Lee was stunned with emotion, but she realized that she must accept the folded envelope and not deny Alfredo the sincere expression of his gift. The moment might have remained private and untold had it not been for the witness who recognized the personal history behind it and wept a few tears with Lee as the elevator ascended to the fourth floor.

27

Kim on Television

IF YOU ARE A BIG-LEAGUE television news anchor or talk show host, one of your producers solicits the people who appear on your show to be interviewed. They tell your guest to keep their answers brief and not to look directly into the camera. They try to calm your guest on the studio set, but most guests are very nervous. You, as host, get a pre-show briefing about your guest, and your teleprompter will probably have the guest's name in large letters and a few lead questions. Usually, your initial contact with your guest is made during the commercial break when introductions are made, and the guest sits in the chair across from your anchor desk and is fitted for his or her lapel microphone. Then you take your seat again as the floor manager counts down the last ten seconds before you go back live on air. You address your personal close-up camera, introduce your guest and topic, ask your lead question, and pray that your guest does not freeze in the camera frame, or even worse, respond to you with a sentence that has no end. You have no problem, however, if your guest is Kim Fisher.

Maybe your show producer didn't know or forgot to reassure you, but Kim Fisher has done hundreds of television interviews, more than a few on the major networks with bigger audiences than yours. Your first impression of the underwater treasure hunter is that he may have just gotten off the salvage boat. The man is very tall, very tanned, and he is wearing shorts, sandals, and a short-sleeve monogrammed Mel Fisher's Treasures shirt. What immediately catches your eye, however, is the long, thick gold chain that he is wearing around his neck and the huge emerald ring on his finger. The guest seems very relaxed. He is also well groomed with a barbered haircut that would befit any Wall Street hedge fund executive. When responsible for millions of dollars, it is best to look stable and reassured. Neatness counts.

Kim Fisher arrived in the studio with a briefcase full of treasure from the *Atocha*, and the artifacts are now displayed on your desk top. They include a golden chalice, gold bars, a surprisingly heavy gold disk, silver reals, and pieces-of- eight dating from 1622, and emerald jewelry. You ask the value of the sample treasure set before you. You cannot stop yourself from raised-eyebrows surprise and a small gasp. The ten or so artifacts are worth millions. The gold chalice alone is valued at over $1 million, and the emerald in the ancient gold setting is worth more than $500,000.

The treasure finder smiles at your reaction. He has witnessed amazement like yours many times. You make eye contact across the desk, and you have the feeling that this man is one of the coolest guys that you've ever met. He's told you his treasure story in almost the fewest words possible, but each answered question contained a punch-line end. Your segment with Kim Fisher made for perfect television. The commercial break arrives, and you stand up and walk around your anchor desk to shake the guest's hand again. This time, however, you really mean it when you thank him. You will remember him for a long, long time and wonder if you could separate yourself from your coat-and-tie existence and wear shorts and sandals most days for the rest of your life. You wonder if you could ever become the kind of risk taker who searches for shipwreck treasure. Maybe you imagine yourself on Kim's salvage boat at sea in search of the *Atocha's* sterncastle. Maybe you even dream about yourself in a permanent Key West adventure.

After the show, you call the producer into your office who booked Kim Fisher.

"Keep your eye on that Fisher guy," you instruct. "When he finds the *Atocha* sterncastle, I want him on my show the very next day. Send a camera crew if you have to, but let's be first on this story. The camera loves this guy, and his story is terrific."

28

The Complex Business
of Treasure Hunting

IT TAKES A BUDGETED $3,600,000 annually to operate a salvage company the size of Mel Fisher's Treasures. With its captains and crews of the two large salvage boats, the 90-ft. motor vessel *JB Magruder* and the 90-ft. research vessel *Dare*, its re-supply-at-sea crafts and crews, its curators and conservators of the artifacts themselves, its retail artifact sales stores and staff, its staff archaeologist, its Spanish archives historian, its Investor Relations specialists, its marketing staff, human resources department, bookkeeping and inventory staff (to name the largest general categories), it is a complex business. The stakes are high for every department manager and every long-term employee because treasure must be found to continue the enterprise. One large-haul treasure season can keep the staff busy for a couple of years, but ultimately, the boats must find and recover something of great value. And when it happens, the cheers echo throughout the Museum building on all four floors, and there is suddenly cold champagne available for the celebration. Kim and Gary Randolph, who joined the company in 1995 as captain of the *JB Magruder* and is now the salvage operations manager and company vice president, report the finds in detail, and then prepare to rush out to the victorious salvage boat in a speedy supply craft. Imagine, if you can, the staff emotions in 1985 when the *Atocha* Mother Lode, valued then at $400 million, was found.

The event was a vindication of everything Mel Fisher and family had envisioned. Kim Fisher today is on the artifact trail of an even larger *Atocha* treasure that was stored in its missing sterncastle. A full 20% of all the gold and silver shipped on the *Atocha* was smuggled by its wealthy passengers, and even members of the king of Spain's royal court, to avoid the king's 20% tax as well as the fees charged by the galleon owners for safe armed passage back to Spain. Then, too, the high Catholic clergy aboard the *Atocha* were not above sequestering their own treasures to avoid the taxation.

Since only the gold and silver bullion was taxed, not jewelry, many passengers wore their wealth in gold chains and fabulous rings and crucifixes. Then, too, the Spanish king was so desperate for the 1622 bullion treasure to save his crown from war-induced bankruptcy that he imposed a 90% forced loan on bullion arriving in Spanish ports from the New World. Instead of riches in the cargo hole, the passengers were left holding IOUs. No wonder the passengers resorted to smuggling.

Mel Fisher had evidence, he claimed, that one of the *Atocha*'s passengers had smuggled an entire chest of high-quality emeralds that he safeguarded in his sterncastle cabin. The value of this extremely large hoard of emeralds could exceed the total amount of everything else on the ship. Mel himself had recovered *Atocha* emeralds valued as much as $600,000 each. Some of the smaller *Atocha* emeralds in a retail setting today demand prices upwards of $20,000. How would you like to be an expedition member for the salvage season that finds the *Atocha* sterncastle and the chest of smuggled emeralds? Imagine taking part in the division of more than $1 billion in Federal Court adjudicated treasure. And figure this—your share of the emeralds and gold and silver are not taxable until you sell them. That is why expedition members are paid by membership points in artifacts rather than cash. There is also a Certificate of Authenticity awarded for each artifact so there is no question of its provenance when offered for sale. The Fisher company can provide an unbroken chain of authenticity by tracking each artifact back to the exact day that it was recovered, which boat recovered it, which crewmember, plus its location site in the ocean. These details confirm which galleon, the *Atocha* or the *Santa Margarita*, provided the specific piece. Artifacts that do not have such bonafide historic certification are greatly reduced in value and may even be manufactured fakes. The adage of "buyer beware" is especially appropriate in the sales arena of Spanish galleon artifacts.

In Eugene Lyon's book, *Search for the Mother Lode of the Atocha*, he noted that Mel Fisher held nothing against salvage rivals even when they had done him harm. Mel wasted little time in anger and spent no energy at all in malice. The same could be true of the son who succeeded him in the family treasure-hunting business—Kim. But where Mel may have been careless in association with ingenuous associates, and expansive in his claims and promises, Kim is a model of reserve and careful in the exercise of his management powers.

29

The Technology of Treasure Hunting

THE HISTORY OF MEL Fisher's Treasures is one filled with innovation and even invention. When obstacles and barriers presented themselves to hinder the discovery of shipwreck treasure, Mel Fisher and his associates initiated solutions that would forever alter the methods of underwater salvaging, and those technical advances continue to this day.

When Mel began searching for the remains of the 1715 Spanish treasure fleet in the waters off Ft. Pierce Inlet on Florida's east coast in 1963, the salvors employed a proton magnetometer and by a grid search "magged" the ocean bottom for hits on ferrous metals. An iron anchor, for example, would draw an anomaly on the graph paper and indicate a site to be explored by divers.

This remarkable advance in locating iron was the genius of Fay Field, who began a 30-year relationship with the Fisher organization. Once the magnetometer had indicated a site of interest, and a marker buoy was dropped, divers had to descend to investigate. Too often the clearer water at the surface became murky and unworkable at the bottom. Divers with very limited visibility had to feel around in the sand and mud like blind men and hope they felt something that they could bring close to their diving masks for identification.

Mel addressed the problem with a common sense question: How can we move the clear water to the bottom so our divers can see? Their solution was ingenious. Mel paired large metal tubes that could be lowered over the props of the salvage boat. They called these stern tubes the "mailboxes" because the first prop wash deflectors resembled oval rural mailboxes. When the mailbox was lowered into the water for the first time from a four-point well-anchored boat, Mel got a pleasant surprise. The prop wash of the boat propelled the clear surface water to the shallow bottom, and voilá, a bubble of visibility was created. But there was an even greater bonus from this invention. The prop-driven column of water also gently dug a large hole in the sand that revealed everything buried beneath.

Prior to the invention of the mailbox, treasure hunters had relied on airlifts or venturi dredges to move the sand. The mailbox could move as much sand in one day as the prior system could in one month. This greatly increased the amount of sea-floor that could be explored each season. The combination of the towable magnetometer and the Fay Fields mailbox invention proved to be the keys to successful treasure hunting.

The first big payoff as the direct result of Mel and Fay's inventions occurred in June 1964. There had been earlier finds of an iron cannon and 100 silver coins in April a short distance from the reef in 12 feet of water. Then 15 pounds of gold disks were recovered in May, but on June 1st, the mailbox uncovered a carpet of gold. There were coins everywhere. Gold coins the size of silver dollars—1,033 of them that day! The next day the mailbox uncovered gold coins in every hole that it created—900 more gold coins with dates ranging from 1699-1715. Has any American invention ever yielded so much profit so fast? The Fisher-Field inventor duo made many people millionaires over the course of their lifetimes.

It is important to remember that in these early years of shipwreck treasure salvaging off the east coast of Florida and the Florida Keys, there was no global positioning system (GPS) and not even the LORAN system for positioning boats at sea. Thus, working a grid pattern in open water was a severe navigational challenge. Boat captains needed to know what had already been magged and explored by the divers so that they could move on to other promising sites. Since the magnetometer registered an anomaly on every ferrous metal object, from Navy practice bombs to meteorites from outer space, it was important to identify those findings on the navigation charts so that they would not come up again.

Time and time again, especially when complicated by shifting winds and ocean currents, salvage boats had difficulty keeping a steady course on their search grid coordinates while towing a mag head 200 ft. behind the vessel. Again, necessity breeds invention, and Mel Fisher was equal to the task. For $1500 each, Mel purchased theodolites, surveying instruments utilizing a telescopic attachment to measure angles. The use of the theodolites was for a crewmember to lock the base of the device on a known compass heading that fixed on an object like a lighthouse. Perched on a tower for the survey day, the theodolite operator could keep a survey boat on a given survey line by directing its helmsman by radio.

Mel had to be inventive in finding spots to locate his theodolite observation towers while out at sea. Once he constructed a platform on the upper-level decking of the Cosgrove Shoal Lighthouse, sixty feet above sea level, with a sweeping view of the Marquesas Keys. When discovered, the Coast Guard forced the survey crew to vacate.

Another time they mounted the theodolite on the exposed deck of a sunken Navy ship, the *Patricia*. With Navy jet bombers en route, the survey crew received a frantic message to abandon their post. The *Patricia* was an active Navy target ship!

Other theodolites were set atop towers made from shrimp boat booms and set up on a shoal that were covered in seagull droppings. The duty was a rotating assignment that did not motivate volunteers. Given a bagged lunch, a cooler of beverages, an umbrella, and a car battery and radio with their theodolite tripod, tower hours in the sun and wind could be very punishing duty. Then, too, when the car-sized radio battery had to be transferred from a supply boat to a tower in a rolling sea, the acrobatics could prove dangerous. And occasionally when the need was great, lights were mounted on the salvage boats, and the magging was run all night.

In the early 1980s, a Del Norte microwave navigation system was installed near the Marquesas where the search for the *Atocha* was concentrated. Two transmitting towers with a receiving station on the salvage boat could triangulate the exact chart position of the boat within three to five feet. Finally, it was technologically easy to return to the mag hit sites. The former theodolite tower survey crew must have rejoiced!

In 2012 a new age of treasure salvage technology began with the development of *Dolores*, a custom-built Hybrid Autonomous Underwater Vehicle (HAUV). Named to honor Dolores Fisher, whose grace and character supported her husband Mel and the entire Fisher family through an amazing half-century of both trag-edy and victory, the HAUV will blaze a great new era of discovery.

The *Dolores* is an inventive development from the talents and skills of Gary Randolph, Vice President and Operations Direc-tor for Mel Fisher's Expeditions, and CEO Kim Fisher. These men are equal to the now legendary personalities who came before them in the 50-year history of their company.

Dolores is capable of side scanning an 800-1000-meter swath of sea floor in a single pass in deep water. She also has an inte-grated magnetometer for detecting shipwrecks in the nadir or "blind spot" directly beneath the side scan sonar. The sonar and magnetometer systems are linked to a computer navigation sys-tem so that every substantial target can be accurately located. In addition, *Dolores* is equipped with an electromagnetic detector, an advanced device that can discriminate the difference between gold and silver and other metals. *Dolores* also has forward-looking sonar, multi-directional cameras, and lights and has the capabil-ity to be connected to the ship via a fiber optic tether in order to conduct target identification operations or to run her grids autonomously. The operations center for *Dolores* in the main cabin of the motor vessel *Dare* resembles a NASA launch control room. Consoles and monitor screens line the main salon, and comfortable executive office chairs are in position for the long hours of directing *Dolores* on the seafloor.

When *Dolores* locates a valuable target that is too deep to be worked by divers, a Remotely Operated Vehicle (ROV) will be needed to do the archaeological survey and recovery. The engi-neering for an ROV "Melvin" has been completed, and several of the longest production time components have been ordered.

Gary Randolph is uniquely qualified to lead development in this new age of shipwreck discovery. He has been part of the

Fisher family company since 1995 when he was made captain of the *JB Magruder*, a principal vessel in the company's salvage fleet. By 1997, he was elevated to Operations Manager. Gary is a large, powerful man with a gentle disposition. His management style among captains, crews, and technicians is inclusive as he leads by example rather than by authority. Gary is jovial when not concentrating on the technology of *Dolores*. He is thus easy to be around and a welcomed working partner.

As the chief of the conservation laboratory, Gary, a computer whiz, developed one of the most comprehensive marine archaeological artifact databases in the world. He has also been an Expedition Leader to sites of full ocean-depth shipwrecks. With twenty years of proven treasure-finding success behind him, you can bet that Gary and *Dolores* will make treasure-recovery history in the near future. With Kim and Gary leading the way, the Fisher company has justified great expectations. Look what Mel and Fay brought up with only a crude magnetometer and a couple of mailboxes!

30

Shawn Redding – Chief Engineer

BOAT CAPTAINS IN THE Fisher company fleet will tell you that Shawn Redding is their M.V.P. He is the one team player that they depend on for the safety and sea worthiness of their boats. From dock to dry dock, to emergency repairs at sea, Shawn is the Chief Engineer in charge of everything mechanical and electrical on the boats. His operational support of the boats, and the deep trust and personal friendships that he maintains with Captains Andy Matroci and José Papo Garcia, is long term.

When Shawn Redding met Mel Fisher in the Key West museum in 1985, the *Atocha* Mother Lode discovery of that July was still at an exciting fever pitch. Nevertheless, Mel took time to interact with Shawn to the extent of inviting him to lift one of the recently recovered heavy silver bars. The personal contact with Mel excited Shawn's imagination, and he returned home to Wilkes County in the Blue Ridge Mountains of North Carolina with the feeling that he must find a way to return to Key West and join the treasure hunting salvaging company. His first commitment was to purchase an expedition membership in the company.

Back in Wilkes County, Shawn had an electrical engineering company to run. He had earned his engineering degree and a master's degree in business administration from Appalachian State University with postgraduate engineering studies at Notre Dame University. In the mid 1990s, his company was perfectly positioned to profit from the rapid expansion of fiber optics in the communications industry. Siecor Corporation, the largest manufacturer of optical fiber cable in the world, was located in Hickory, North Carolina within Shawn's sphere of operations, and his company became a preferred contractor for the installation and development of fiber optic networks. Within a five-year span of fiber optic expansion, Shawn and his associates built a sizeable company.

Shawn then made a decision to step back from the demands of running a big business, although his association with the company that he co-founded continued. He accepted a position as a professor of electrical engineering at Wilkes Community College in his native home area. The job emphasis change then allowed Shawn to satisfy his urge to return to Key West. When the academic year ended in May, he headed for Key West where his engineering expertise was welcomed on the Fisher company boat dock.

Shawn was a certified scuba diver, and soon he was named captain of the 29-foot *Huntress*, a fast 40-knots resupply and workboat. The North Carolina mountain man had a variety of jobs during those college-teaching summer vacation years in Key West. He performed maintenance on the workboats, dove with the expedition members on the *Atocha* site, and he also led excursions to Emerald City to work the sluice boxes for Atocha emeralds. On his own dives, Shawn found both silver coins and emeralds.

"It's always the hope of what you might find in the next hole that keeps you diving year after year," Shawn says. "Mel knew exactly how to fire your imagination in that way."

In 2007 Shawn retired from college teaching and relocated his family to Key West to work full-time with the Fisher company salvors. His home in the old town is only a seven-minute walk to the Greene Street museum office. Most of his time, however, is spent on the boats working directly with the captains on maintenance and upkeep. For taking expedition members out to the boats at sea, Shawn currently drives the *Kingfisher*, a 29-foot Pro-Line center console powerboat, or the *Huntress*.

"Shawn Redding can fix anything," Captain Andy Matroci says. "When I've got an electrical or mechanical problem, I call Shawn on my cellphone from the boat as soon as we are within range; and often by the time I tie up, he has the repair part sitting on the dock. And another thing, Shawn always negotiates the best price possible on anything that he buys for the company. He is shameless when he bargains for price."

Shawn Redding is a big, powerfully built man with an easygoing approachable nature. He is quick to laugh and to swap a story or a joke. He has the kind of "old school" work ethic and

31

A Taste of Fame

IN OCTOBER OF 2013, Joe Sweeney scheduled a week's vacation at the most beautiful beach house on its side of the island in Rincon, Puerto Rico. The use of the house was a gift from another one of Joe's many Jersey Shore friends, and the plan was a guys-only week of charter-boat fishing and relaxation. Kim overheard Joe making travel arrangements with friends included on the trip, and he surprised Joe by asking to be included.

After the first day of fishing and telling sea stories to their charter-boat captain Pepe, the vacationing men returned to the dock and proceeded on their way to drinks and dinner with no public notice. Pepe had told Kim that Mel was especially remembered by the Rincon natives for his generosity and kindness during his treasure-hunting days in Puerto Rican waters. Evidently, Pepe spread the word that Mel's son was on the island.

The next afternoon when Joe's fishing party returned to the dock, a crowd of about 150 men, women, and children were waiting to see and greet the son of the famous Mel Fisher. Kim was very surprised to see all the people waiting for the boat to arrive, and then even more surprised when he discovered that they were waiting for him. While his housemates watched, Kim shook every hand that was extended to him and responded to every question that he could understand in Spanish. He was occupied in the marina parking lot for more than an hour as if he were a pop music star. Pepe told Joe that the people wanted their children to meet Kim because he was the connection to all the stories that they had told about Mel, who was legendary in their minds.

The image of the very tall American being surrounded by an adoring throng of dark-complexioned native Puerto Ricans could easily be a *National Geographic* moment. For Kim, it was a taste of fame.

Mel Fisher and star performer Jimmy Buffett sit
on a pile of silver bars that famous day in July
1985 when the Atocha Mother Lode was found.

Captain Kim Fisher, the teenage treasure hunter.

Kim and Lee on their wedding day.

Photo by Lee Fisher

Kim's five sons with their dad.
(l to r) Jeremy, Sean, Scott, Neko, Kim, and Ricky.

Lee's parents Victor and May Wiegand.

Kim and Lee on an Alaskan adventure.

One of the annual family Christmas card
photos with Scott, Kim, Ricky, and Lee.

Photo by Bob Fontaine

The Atocha Mother Lode Golden Crew Ring was presented by Mel and Deo Fisher to only 84 individuals in April 1987.

Lee shows a giant Atocha emerald being appraised in the offices of the famed emerald expert Manuel Marcial.

Kim appears by Skype on the Huffington Post Live (Feb. 5, 2015) in a show devoted to The Quest for Buried Treasure.

The famous 200 Greene Street address that houses the Mel Fisher Maritime Heritage Museum and the head-quarters of Mel Fisher's Treasures.

Kim works the bottom with a metal detector.

The moment of discovery is a thrill that lasts a lifetime.

Working the airlift on a treasure hunt.

Josh Fisher Abt, son of Michael and Taffi Fisher Abt and grandson of Mel (center), displays the great discovery of a large silver plate with Captain Papo Garcia (right).

Jean Thornton celebrates the
recovery of a large Atocha emerald.

An underwater motion picture photographer shoots one of the
many documentaries focused on Mel Fisher's Treasures.

The artifacts of discovery, like this ceramic jar, are
important archaeological treasures.

JB Magruder crewmember Tony Novelli
holds an encrusted dagger that will require a
great deal of conservation to restore.

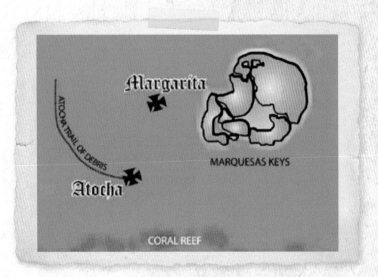

The treasure map.

A diver takes his turn surveying the
seabed for more Atocha treasure.

Dolores is the custom built Hybrid Autonomous
Underwater Vehicle (HAUV) that is destined to
revolutionize shipwreck treasure hunting.

Gary Randolph and Kim Fisher gather with crewmembers
and technicians to welcome Dolores on the deck of the Dare.

4 Cobalt Marine, LLC

9:88
FRI MAY 05

Vice President Gary Randolph at the Dolores
command center on board the M/V Dare.

Treasures of the Nuestra Señora de Atocha on display.

Expedition members work the inflow of the sluice box in search of emeralds at sea on the Emerald City site.

Six happy treasure finders have stories to tell. (l to r) Rose Dirkes, Bob Dirkes, Tom Boesch, C. J. Rhoades, Tim Rhoades (kneeling).

C. J. Rhoades shows off a very sizeable emerald find.

Jim Ford (standing) and wife Ann (on bench)
compare notes for their next dive.

A lady returns up the M/V Dare's dive ladder.

Marta Anys Napoleone is all smiles on the dive boat.

Jean Thornton, Debbie Sexton, and Bob
"Cannonball" Erickson on deck between dives.

Thumbs up for divers Kerry Johnson and
Jason Henthorne ready to go treasure hunting.

Finding an Atocha silver piece-of-eight is always exciting.

The M/V Dare anchored for operations at sea.

The MV JB Magruder anchored on the
Atocha site and ready for operations.

The Mel Fisher Days pub crawl always draws a crowd.

The Mel Fisher Days throng on Duval
Street passes a Key West landmark.

The Treasure Booty Bingo Party during Mel Fisher Days in Key West draws a crowd.

Winners of the Mel Fisher Days Treasure Hunt Anthony Porcelli and Kiana Porcelli hold their prize of 5,000 silver dollars as members of team "Monsteras Deliciosas" with Margot Koch and Shawn Griffin.

Kim and Lee in costume for Mel Fisher Days.

Taffi Fisher Abt and Sue Hawkins enjoy Mel Fisher Days.

Captain Andy Matroci and wife Monica on Duval Street for Mel Fisher Days.

MEL FISHER Days   9/17/13   1405
                                                    Date
Pay to the
Order of   WESLEY HOUSE FAMILY SERVICES $20,000
TWENTY THOUSAND AND 0/100 Dollars
:0123456781 4398571: 01405   THE FISHER FAMILY

Kim and Lee present the Mel Fisher Days charity donation to Wesley House Family Services.

Lee and Kim enjoy a private moment at the 2014 Gala.

Guests dine under a sea of lights
at the Division Week Gala.

Division Week begins with a reception in the Mel Fisher
Maritime Museum courtyard. Guests shown here (l to r)
are Michael Piscotty, Bob Dirkes, Mark Long, Rose Dirkes,
Sylvia Van Dyke, and Becky Debaugh.

Guests enjoy a Division Week
party at the Key West Aquarium.

Photo by Sheel Sheelman

Shawn Cowles on stilts poses with guests at the 2014 Gala.

Esther Knapicius and costumed partner Michael Piscotty pose
with Lee and Kim as winners of the Division Week Gala costume contest with Shawn Cowles in the background.

Sylvia Van Dyke and Craig Friberg,
runners-up in the costume contest with Kim
and Lee on the Casa Marina beach.

Erin Uzume McKenna goes all out in
costuming for the Division Week Gala.

Bob and Margo Carey as King and Queen
Neptune attend the 2014 Gala.

Photo by Carol Tedesco

Jim and Ann Ford pose with Kim and Lee at the 2014 Gala.

Photo by Carol Tedesco

Key West singer Bria Ansara joins
the 2014 Gala costume parade.

Dr. Eugene Lyon: Most Valuable Historian

IN KNOWING THE FISHER family history for finding Spanish galleon treasure, you obviously recognize Dr. Eugene Lyon as the quintessential New World Spanish colonial historian and archival researcher who made the discoveries possible. The story of how Eugene Lyon and his wife Dot met Mel and Deo Fisher is a lesson on the virtues of attending Sunday School, because that is where they met according to the legend. You may, therefore, be tempted to believe that Dr. Lyon, at age 85, has passed through his glory days and that he has ceased perusing ancient Spanish script in crumbling old documents for yet unclaimed treasure ships. You'd be wrong.

In recent years, Dr. Lyon has delivered documentation on eleven more treasure ships to the Fisher company. And if you dare to think him not up to date, consider that his home computer has been adapted to give him real-time images of what a deepwater ROV sees with its cameras. He is able to view exactly what the salvors in the ship control room are seeing. You might then say that Dr. Lyon is still very much involved in treasure hunting although he does it from the comfort of his home in Vero Beach, Florida.

"My wife does not want me to go to sea anymore," Dr. Lyon says.

There is a very important precedent for why Dr. Lyon heeds his wife's advice. The year was 1952, and Eugene Lyon was a quartermaster and helmsman on the *USS Hobson*, DMS-26, a famous Navy destroyer-minesweeper warship. Commissioned in early 1942, the *Hobson* earned six battle stars for combat action in the North African campaign, fire support off Utah Beach at Normandy, and then action in the Pacific war against Japan. The *Hobson* was part of the invasion fleet that hit Okinawa. It was the greatest amphibious operation ever undertaken, and kamikaze attacks finally laid a

Dr. Eugene Lyon

bomb on *Hobson's* main deck. She was forced to return via the Panama Canal to the Norfolk Naval Shipyard for repairs. Then the war ended.

By the time of the Korean War, Navy helmsman Eugene Lyon was near the end of his term of service. Those years, 1950-51,

Hobson had carrier escort duty off the coast of North Carolina and Puerto Rico. The ship's next cruise would be a cushy one, the kind that every sailor dreams about: the Mediterranean with 20 exotic ports of call. Gene was offered a promotion in rank if he would extend his term of service for six months and make the Med cruise. Dot, however, was about to graduate from Florida State University, and she was pulling on Gene's heartstrings. The decision was made. Gene would leave the Navy, and they would soon be married.

The USS *Hobson* sailed without its 23-year-old helmsman Gene Lyon; and on April 26, 1952, steaming in escort formation with the aircraft carrier *Wasp* (CV-18), the *Wasp* turned to reposition itself for the recovery of aircraft. The two escort ships could lag behind the turn, or they could cross its bow. The night was dark, and by human error, the *Hobson* attempted to cross the bow of the *Wasp*. The huge carrier then struck the destroyer amidship, and the force of the collision rolled the *Hobson* until it broke in two. The *Hobson* sank in four minutes. 176 sailors, including their captain, perished. The *Wasp* recovered 61 survivors. Many of the lost were known to Gene as shipmates. Today, after more than 60 years of marriage, Dr. Lyon believes that he would have died on the *Hobson* if he had not come ashore to marry Dot.

As a native Floridian, Gene Lyon spent his first post-college years as a city manager for Vero Beach. Then he began to teach history at the local community college. His abiding interest in the Spanish conquest of Florida led him to return to graduate school in 1967 to study for a doctorate in Latin American history. At the University of Florida a collection of handwritten scripts from the "Archives of the Indies" were available to review on microfilm. It was here Gene learned to read the 17th-century Spanish documents. It was this skill, to read and translate archaic ship-related manifests and reports, that would make him indispensable to the treasure hunting industry. Gene's next step was to go to Seville, Spain to do research for his Ph.D dissertation on Florida's Spanish origins at the Archive of the Indies where he could physically hold the original manifests. He would eventually spend a total of six years researching in Spain and thinks of Seville as his second home.

When Mel and Deo, who had been church friends with the Lyons for about five years, learned that they were going to Spain in 1969 for a year, Mel asked Gene to look into the Spanish archival documents for evidence of the 1622 *Nuestra Señora de Atocha* and *Santa Margarita* shipwrecks. Although many competitors (some with associates already working the Archive of the Indies) were searching, no location had yet been identified.

Being fluent in modern Spanish, and having a working knowledge of archaic abbreviations and the older vocabulary, allowed Gene to understand the language of the 16th and 17th-century documents in the Seville archives; yet, many challenges still lay ahead. The more considerable problems were the damages of age, as many of these 400-year-old bundled documents are charred and brittle, or riddled with wormholes.

The unbroken cursive scrawl resembling Arabic or Gothic had very little punctuation, and the ancient terminology used back then required additional skills to decipher the information. The patience and skill of locating useful archival information, and then translating it for historical evaluation, is the work of a serious scholar.

Gene's first significant find was the original manifest of the 1622 fleet that detailed for the king's tax purposes the cargoes lost in the *Atocha* and *Santa Margarita* shipwrecks. The Spanish were meticulous and fastidious record keepers throughout the centuries of building their colonial empire; and without their obsession to document, trails to Spanish galleon shipwrecks would not exist. Gene reported the details of the super-rich 1622 fleet cargoes to Mel, and that February, Mel and Deo flew to Spain and surprised Gene by visiting him at the Archive of the Indies. Their excitement was high; but ten days later, after Deo and Mel had returned to Florida, Gene called with information that would change history. He had located a key piece of the puzzle that no other treasure salvor possessed.

The document that proved to send the Fisher company into a new and ultimately successful direction was titled, "Accounts of Francisco Nuñez Melián, of what he salvaged from the galleon Margarita . . . in the Keys of Matecumbe, coast of Florida." The title alone caused Gene's heart to race. The document proved to be rich in detail, and it described the four-year effort to recover the *Santa Margarita*'s treasure. At the end of his study of the document, Gene had an aha moment of realization. Mel and his salvor competitors had been looking for the *Santa Margarita* and the *Atocha* in the wrong place; in fact, they were 100 miles off course.

The salvors were searching for the *Atocha* off Matecumbe Key in Florida because that name was often noted in the documents of 1622. But at the time of the shipwrecks, the term "Matecumbe" was generic and referred to all the Florida Keys except for the Tortuga group. In later documents, the Marquis of Cadereita was shown to have commissioned Gaspar de Vargas to find and salvage the lost 1622 ships. In February 1623 the Marquis became impatient with the lack of salvage results and left Havana for the Keys to lead the salvage operation in person. He established his base camp at a group of low mangrove islands near the shipwreck sites. Salvage master Gaspar de Vargas then honored the fleet commander by naming the islands Cayos del

Marques – "Keys of the Marquis." With this revelation, Gene then located the Marquesas Keys on modern charts. It was very clear to him that the *Atocha* and the *Santa Margarita* should be found in the vicinity of the Marquesas Keys. The futures of many individuals turned on that moment of realization by Gene Lyon, not the least, his own.

Dr. Lyon as author and historian has created an enduring document of his own, titled *Search for the Mother Lode of the Atocha*. The trade paperback edition published in 1989 by Florida Classics Library includes ancient and contemporary foldout salvors charts. The reproduction of the modern chart is 14 x 18 inches, and it pinpoints all the major treasure sites including those of the *Santa Margarita* and the *Atocha* Mother Lode. The narrative story is very well told, but there is a huge bonus of fascinating detail contained in the nine appendices to the book.

Appendix A is the paper that Dr. Lyon delivered to the Society of Historical Archaeology titled "Atocha: What Documents Told" in January 1987. Other appendices include Dr. Lyon's translations of communications to the Spanish crown by agents reporting the shipwreck and salvage circumstances of 1622 and 1623.

Appendix F, however, may be the most compelling to modern readers because it lays bare the nitty-gritty of the treasure salvage business. The text is the Finding of Fact in a dispute over salvage rights to the treasure of the *Santa Margarita*. The case was litigated in the U.S. District Court, Southern District of Florida, with the eminent Senior Federal Judge James Lawrence King presiding. The events in question occurred in May 1980. The judgment was not rendered until January 1983. Judge King quoted liberally from the writing of Dr. Lyon in his summation of the case.

Dr. Lyon's identification with the *Atocha* and *Santa Margarita* treasures is further documented in five separate *National Geographic* articles. He also has two *National Geographic* cover features, "Search for Columbus" (Jan. 1992) and "The Manila Galleons" (Sept. 1990). He is also the author of five books. As the pre-eminent scholar on Spanish colonial Florida and the Spanish maritime system, his many honors and awards include Official in the Order of Isabella as conferred by King Juan Carlos of Spain; Comendador in the Order of Christopher Columbus as con-ferred by the President of the Dominican Republic; The Order of Florida as presented by the City of St. Augustine as its highest honor; The Jillian Prescott Award for Lifetime Service by the Florida Historical Society (2003); and the Mel Fisher Lifetime Achievement Award (2005). Dr. Lyon considers his most pres-tigious award to be the 2011 Dorothy Dodd Lifetime Achieve-ment Award given by the Florida Historical Society.

Did Dr. Lyon get rewarded for his key role in finding the *Ato-cha* and the *Margarita*? The answer is yes, handsomely. He earned treasure divisions as both a company stockholder and expedition member that were valued in the hundreds of thousands of dol-lars. Dr. Lyon then chose to donate a large portion of his treasure to the University of Florida and the 4-H Foundation.

A number of his *Atocha* coins were soon spent to build a swimming pool behind the Lyons' Vero Beach home. Then, too, with three daughters and a son who have law degrees and Ph.D's among them, you have to figure that treasure also paid for a lot of formal education.

Today, while any of their six grandsons play in the back yard swimming pool, Gene can watch them from his reading chair. If you come for a visit, he may want to talk to you about the char-acter and accomplishments of Thomas Jefferson. He has just

Andy Matroci: The Man Who Saw It All

FEW INDIVIDUALS OTHER THAN members of the Fisher family themselves have endured the trials and triumphs of Mel Fisher's Treasures longer or more directly than diver and boat captain Andy Matroci.

Andy grew up on Lake Michigan in Chicago. He became a certified diver at Triton College and then a dive instructor by age 19. By 1975, he received his commercial dive certification at Ocean Corporation in Houston, Texas. He then worked difficult and dangerous underwater jobs until exhausted in 1981, he sought the relief of a vacation. Andy headed for Key West to relax in the warm Florida waters, and did what else? He hung out with divers for some recreation diving.

Captain Billy Deans became a close friend on that trip and introduced Andy to the concept of diving for shipwreck treasure. Andy says that he never imagined that a diver could earn a living by searching for treasure. The obvious next step was to meet Mel

Fisher, America's most famous diver and treasure hunter, in an environment where Andy could see for himself the gold and silver artifacts recovered from the Florida wreck of the 1715 Spanish fleet and the 1622 sinking of the galleon *Santa Margarita*. The greatest prize, however, Mel told Andy, was the fabled *Atocha*. Mel told Andy that his company was following the *Atocha*'s trail and that the discovery of its Mother Lode was expected any day.

Captain Andy Matroci in the wheel house of the M/V Magruder

When Andy presented his formal résumé as a commercial diver, Mel laughed and said that it was the first one he had ever seen. He then offered Andy a diving job at $103 per week, a figure well below what Andy earned in a single day on his commercial jobs. But the excitement that Mel was so famous for inciting infected Andy, and two weeks later Andy quit his high-paying commercial diving job and relocated from Chicago to Key West. Andy told his friends and family that he would try treasure hunting for only a year.

"I could not have lived with myself if I had refused Mel and then read later about the discovery of the *Atocha* Mother Lode. Mel gave me a career that I never knew existed, and 35 years later, I'm still treasure hunting."

Andy, as the newcomer, was assigned as a diver on Kane Fisher's boat, but his professionalism did not impress the Fisher captains or crews. Then, during the mid-summer of their 1981 operations, Andy brought up two gold bars, which he placed into the hands of Kim Fisher. Suddenly, Andy was a made man, a diver who had the skill or the luck of actually finding treasure. Everyone profits when treasure arrives from the sea bottom to the salvage boat deck.

But Andy wanted to do more than just dive, and he was troubled by the fact that he never knew his chart location when at sea. He asked Syd Jones, then captain of the company's *Swordfish*, to teach him the basics of underwater archaeology and the Del Norte navigation system. Andy soon became adept at keeping charts and plotting the areas that the salvage vessels had worked. By late 1983, he had logged 20 months of recording data on the ship's charts, and he came to agree with Kane on the best plot line for finding the *Atocha* Mother Lode. It was not a theory shared by Mel and the other boat captains who were still finding occasional gold bars and silver coins in the relatively shallow Quicksands site. Most captains wanted nothing to do with searches in deep water.

In 1983 Kane, as captain of the *Dauntless,* navigated between the Marquesas and the Quicksands on a course toward deeper water than where the Bank of Spain glory hole, the *Atocha* cannons, and the *Atocha* anchor were found. Andy Matroci was the boat's first mate at the time. Kane Fisher, the youngest of Mel's three sons, was obstinate in his view of where to search for the

Atocha, but he was not forthcoming with his crew. From 1983, throughout the next 18 months, the *Dauntless* slowly worked down a course line in 45-ft. meticulous circle searches. With two-man dive teams searching the bottom holes made by the twin prop wash deflectors, the results were very disappointing. No treasure or any sign of the *Atocha* was found.

By the summer of 1984, despite treasure being recovered from the *Santa Margarita* by other company vessels, the company had exhausted its capital funding, and Mel Fisher had no choice but to lay off most of his diving crews. While the excavated treasure was tied up in court cases, captains and crews saw no regular paydays, and some resorted to food stamps as a way to feed their families. Mel instructed his son Kane to abandon his deep-water search and concentrate on the still productive Quicksands, but Kane stubbornly continued to make detours to his search line that became known as "Kane's Trail."

In the fall of 1984, Mel's mind was changed, however, when Kane's divers found telling artifacts that included square spikes known to have been used on the doomed *Atocha*. Suddenly, all the company's salvage assets and energy focused on the deep-water direction. Andy was a key participant in the trials and challenges of those critical months, and he would be rewarded for his dedication by participating firsthand in the ultimate discovery.

On Memorial Day weekend 1985, Andy was assigned as a diver on the large and powerful 170-foot M/V *Saba Rock*, an added salvage boat contracted from its homeport in New Orleans. Whenever Mel contracted for extra salvage vessels and equipped them with "mailboxes," the twin prop wash deflectors, he wanted his own people in the crew to account for any treasures that might be found. On this particular day, Andy's dive partner, Greg Wareham, had been recalled to another boat, and

Andy found himself the lone professional diver on the *Saba Rock* with its captain, Ed Stevens, and Ed's fiancée, Susan Nelson.

The big boat was so powerful, and its twin screws were far enough apart, that its mailboxes could produce two blowholes at a single revving of the engines, one port and one starboard. Ed did not like to blow two holes at a time because of the additional fuel consumption, but Andy convinced him to start their dive day by blowing two holes. He would search one hole while Susan searched the other. Susan was late getting into her dive gear, so Andy hit the water first.

He descended straight down to the portside chasm in the sand 50 feet below the surface and went to his knees to adjust his loop metal detector. As soon as it was tuned in, it began to sound the alert. Andy pushed away the sand to discover that he was kneeling on a carpet of silver coins.

The odds-defying moment of diving directly on treasure was interrupted by Susan who had dived on his hole instead of

Captain Andy searches the charts for treasure sites.

the one assigned to her. When she tapped Andy on the shoulder, he turned to see her holding a bar of solid gold. When she swam down to him, she had noticed something yellow just under the extension of his fins as he knelt collecting the coins. She said later that she thought it was some yellow plastic trash stuck to his fins, but when she grabbed it, it was gold—one of five gold bars lying at Andy's feet! She was inexperienced, and she was in the wrong hole, but that didn't make any difference to the reporters who all wanted to interview the girl who found the gold bars. That day, both Andy and Ed Stevens were regarded as bystanders.

With the discovery of the 13 gold bars and many coins, the next day promised more excitement. By rights, as the senior diver, Andy could have commanded the first hole of the day, and he was ready to hit the water when Syd Jones and his wife K.T. (Fisher company divers since 1981) arrived on the scene by boat. The young adventurous couple were returning from a trip abroad, and they were eager to get back into the water. Generously, Andy gave them the first dive of the day. When they surfaced from their exploration of the bottom, Syd asked Andy to help him with his troubled regulator. It was the setup for a joke. Syd and K.T. had found a dozen small pieces of gold-and-emerald jewelry that a wealthy Spanish lady might have worn on her dress, and they had packed them below the cap of Syd's regulator. With the cap removed, Syd emptied the cache of jewelry into the palms of Andy's hands. They were treasures Andy would have found if he had not allowed them to dive first. For the second day in a row, great treasure had been recovered in a hole that should have been Andy's!

Kane insisted on going further east-southeast from the productive glory hole along Hawk Channel by leap-frogging along a two-mile line of buoys. Kane had persisted on a deep-water theory regarding the *Atocha,* and his divers were now diving on blowholes at a depth of 54 feet of water. Late in the afternoon of the 19th of July, Kane brought up a ballast stone, an olive jar neck, and a barrel hoop. On deck of the *Dauntless*, Andy sighted a four-reales blackened sulfide coin that had escaped notice. There were three more encrusted to the barrel hoop. Immediately back in the water, Kane saw hundreds of silver coins scattered across the hole blown in the bottom. None of the six-member crew slept much, and they were back on the dive site soon after dawn.

All boats were now working Kane's Trail in a southeastern line running from the treasure-rich Quicksands to the outer reef. Kim Fisher commanded the *Bookmaker* and magged the area. Divers from the *Swordfish*, captained by Tom Ford, found a 17th-century swivel gun. The excitement on all boats was electric as they anticipated making history with each successive dive.

On history's most triumphant shipwreck treasure discovery day, the *Saba Rock* had returned to harbor with engine problems. *Dauntless* and *Swordfish* leap-frogged down Kane's Trail. The Fisher company office remained on high alert since the discovery of the square spikes, and the silver coin-studded barrel hoops led everyone to believe that the discovery of the *Atocha* Mother Lode was imminent. All the Fisher salvage resources were now focused on a single search area. *Dauntless* and *Swordfish* were joined by *Bookmaker* and *Virgalona*.

On the 20th, the day's first hole was made by the *Dauntless* as its big funnel tubes were lowered over the ship's props. The first set of divers found coins, pottery, and more barrel hoops. At around 11 a.m. the second diving pair surfaced with handfuls of blackened silver pieces-of-eight. Then the third hole of the day was blown, and Andy and Greg Wareham (age 26 from Dubuque, Iowa) took their dive turn.

Before they entered the water, Andy told Greg that he wanted them to explore southeast from the hole. Whatever was exposed in the hole (silver plates, silverware, copper ingots, and hundreds of coins) could wait until they swam out about 100 feet in search of a greater treasure. Andy used his underwater compass to point the direction, and the two divers swam a parallel course over a rippled sand bottom. The waters were cloudy and dark, so they soon lost visual contact with each other. When Andy judged that he had reached the extent of his exploration, he turned around to swim back to the hole.

Meanwhile, Greg had come across a huge clump, a reef-like mass, emerging from the shadows. His heart racing, he came closer to see the rotted remains of ship's timbers and its precious cargo laid out in the sand and mud. Visibility was no more than eight feet. Greg resisted the impulse to explore an exposed chest full of coins and swam back to find Andy. Greg's frantic gestures and bulging eyes urged Andy to follow him, and the two divers converged on the low, gray reef that appeared amid sponges and lobsters who had made the artificial reef their home.

The reef stack looked like blackened loaves of bread, but both divers recognized that the loaves were silver bars stacked atop each other. The dimensions proved to be staggering: the solid silver reef was four feet tall, 20 feet wide, and 75 feet long. Then, too, there were thousands of silver coins scattered in the sand around the mass of the silver bars. Andy lifted one of the 80-pound bars to his kneecaps but then replaced it. He bit through his rubber mouthpiece as he tried to shout through the escaping air bubbles. "Silver bars! Silver bars!"

Andy realized they had found the Mother Lode, and that once they reached the surface and announced it to the world, the site would never again be the same. After they had cavorted like children and hugged in celebration, Andy signaled for the two of them to calm down. He motioned for Greg to follow him in two wide circles of the silver reef and its treasure chests. The moment of discovery was theirs to see and savor in a quiet and calm that would soon enough be broken.

Usually when divers surface from a blow hole, they are very near their dive boat; but when Andy and Greg came up, they were about 100 feet from the *Dauntless* with the *Swordfish* positioned between them. Andy remembers shouting, "It's here! It's here! The Mother Lode!" Suddenly the water was filled with divers from every boat. By the time Andy climbed back aboard the *Dauntless*, there was only one girl left on deck to greet him. Everybody else was in the water.

Despite a storm that moved in and pelted the crews with hard rain and churned the sea into five-foot waves, treasure fever infected everyone. The sons of Mel Fisher felt the release of the 16 years that their father had preached, "Today's the day." Finally the day had come.

Andy had been on the VHF radio to Mel when he had finally been found shopping and returned to the office. Andy could hear the uproar of the office people as they celebrated. Mel and others would soon rush by their fastest resupply boat to join the excitement on board the *Dauntless*.

Kane wanted to hoist up as many silver bars as he could so that his father could sit on a silver throne, but Andy reminded him that Mel had an exclusive contract with National Geographic to film the recovery. Nevertheless, enough bars were brought up to build a chair for Mel and celebration guest Jimmy Buffett to sit on, play guitar, and toast with champagne.

There was also a concern to honor the archaeological integrity of the wreck site, and Duncan Mathewson would soon be on board to direct the scientific documentation of the discovery. But in the first hours, no one could stop the harvest of the Mother Lode. On the *Dauntless*, the crew started a spontaneous bucket brigade by attaching ropes to buckets, and even milk crates, in order to hoist the heavy silver bars from the bottom. The frenzy went on for hours until Mel, on the radio, ordered Andy to immediately stop all treasure recovery.

Finally, at about four in the afternoon, the hardship of the stormy waters and the physical exhaustion of the crew ended the salvage frenzy, but not before 175 bars of silver, almost eight tons, were stacked on the deck of the *Dauntless*. The boat itself was listing badly from the load and was riding so low in the water that it was in danger of sinking. To prevent that disaster, the crews that evening transferred half of the treasure to the *Swordfish* and dispersed the weight by stacking the bars below decks.

The great discovery day was Saturday, July 20, 1985, ten years to the day since the tragic deaths of Dirk and Angel Fisher and Rick Gage. That serious reflection was overshadowed by the general chaos and excitement of the moment by most people with the exception of the Fisher family.

Soon treasure fever turned into media madness as networks and publications reported the astonishing *Atocha* story. *National Geographic* divers with film cameras converged on the silver bar reef. *The New York Times*, *Time Magazine*, *Newsweek*, *U.S. News*, and *Life* made Mel Fisher their front page and cover story. Mel was quoted as saying "fantabulous" over and over again. Mel was then rushed to New York to appear on the big three network morning talk shows. Summoned to Hollywood, Mel appeared on Johnny Carson's top-rated *Tonight Show*. The following month, Carson came to Key West to personally dive on the *Atocha*.

Andy Matroci will tell you today that getting rich from treasure was never his dream. When he was a kid, he dreamed of playing major league baseball. When he received his divisions from the 1715 Fleet, the *Santa Margarita*, and the *Atocha*, Andy preferred to reserve most of his gold and silver for its future use in fulfilling his own dreams that included marriage and family, and perhaps a secure retirement after his wanderlust for world travel had been satisfied.

In 1991 Andy was the captain of the *Dauntless*. His vessel was docked, and he was occupied in repairing the outboard engine of its crew motorboat that sat in the water. He remembers the scene well. His hands were greasy and filled with motor parts when Duncan Mathewson called down to him from the dock. Andy was 37 years old that year, and his love for adventure travel had not been fulfilled. He came to offer Andy an opportunity to be the leader of a great worldwide diving adventure called the Pilar Project.

"It's time you leave Mel," Mathewson said. For the next ten years, Andy became a mixed-gas deepwater dive master and project director for the recovery of shipwrecks in Guam, the Philippines, Anguilla, Panama, Honduras, and Ecuador. His passion for travel was being fulfilled; but Andy, now married with children, came to regret the time away from his wife Monica, his daughter Melissa, and his son Andy junior. The project work kept him in foreign ports four months a year and on other jobs the rest of the year. It was a very tiring schedule.

Off Cocos Island on Guam's southern coast, the *Nuestra Señora del Pilar* was enroute from Acapulco, Mexico to an annual trade fair in Manila, Philippines. On June 2, 1690, the Spanish galleon struck the Cocos reef, tore out its bottom, and sank in ocean water at depths between 30 to 87 feet. The Spanish court of inquiry reported that the *Nuestra Señora del Pilar* was carrying as much as $1.2 billion (today's dollars) in Spanish coins as ballast in the lower decks of her hold. That sunken hull then broke apart during subsequent typhoons, and the treasure drifted and scattered into deeper waters.

The Pilar Project began in 1991 when the government of Guam granted salvaging rights to John Bent and a group of investors in Australia. Guam would retain 25% of whatever was recovered from the *Pilar*. Bent then hired undersea archaeologist Duncan Mathewson and master diver Andy Matroci to lead the search. The Discovery Channel featured the Pilar Project in its documentary *Science Frontiers* series.

The Pacific path of the great Spanish galleon ships that lasted for 250 years (1565-1815) was very similar to the seasonal treasure fleets that were represented by the *Santa Margarita* and the *Atocha* who crossed the Atlantic from Havana. From Acapulco, the Spanish galleons laden with silver coins minted in Mexico, Peru, and Bolivia crossed the Pacific, stopping for fresh water at Guam, and continuing to Manila, Philippines, which was the Spanish hub for trade with Asia.

In Manila the silver was exchanged for porcelain, jade, and jewelry from China, silk and art works from Japan, precious stones from India, and spices from Southeast Asia. The Pacific goods were then taken back to Acapulco and transported overland to the galleons like the *Atocha* that would carry them across the Atlantic to the Spanish homeland.

In 1990 Phillip Masters, while researching in the Archive of the Indies in Seville, had discovered documents relating to an official inquiry into the sinking of the *Pilar*. Masters was a historian at the University of Florida, a background similar to Eugene Lyon who had been key to finding the *Atocha*. The Spanish reports indicated that only 5,000 pesos worth of silver coins could be salvaged. The crew of 120, and the 43 soldiers and 22 Franciscan missionaries traveling as passengers were all saved, but the bulk of the *Pílar's* cargo was reported lost.

The diving season in Guam is like the season in the Florida Keys. It runs from May through August due to the risk of typhoons in the Pacific and hurricanes in the Atlantic and generally rough seas during the rest of the year. In the beginning of the search for the *Pílar*, Andy and his divers were searching a hard bottom in 40 to 50 feet of water where clear visibility went to 200 feet. Andy had a habit of scouting areas beyond where his divers were working a search area. He called them "exploring walks." The trail that Andy followed yielded over 2,000 artifacts, including 36 Spanish silver coins minted in Mexico City, Lima, and Potosi in Bolivia before 1690, the year the *Pílar* sank.

The trail, however, led into ever-deeper waters. At 80 feet, divers found hundreds of musket balls. The hard bottom then became broken by deep crevasses. Andy concluded that the *Pílar* had been swept along the hard bottom until it settled into one of the deep crevasses along the artifact trail. Over the centuries, layers of sand and dead coral had covered the treasure. Searching at a depth of 160 feet, the trail spilled over into much deeper water that was too deep for normal operations. The search season ended, and Andy pondered his options.

To continue the search, the company would have to provide expensive ROV (Remotely Operated Vehicle) technology or train a team of divers in deep-water mixed-gas diving. Back in Key West, Andy consulted Billy Deans, one of the top mixed-gas dive masters in the world, to give him an estimate of what it would cost to assemble and train ten divers in deep-water operations. Andy then presented the investors with an all-inclusive budget to train the divers in Key West and put them on site in Guam.

The go-ahead came back almost immediately, and Andy took the 14-day very intensive mixed-gas training with his divers, although he had been certified in past years. And when they left Key West enroute to Guam, Billy Deans was with them as their start-up consultant. He then stayed on the job for the rest of the dive season.

In the Pacific waters off Guam, deep dives into 210 feet of water began to be rewarded with ballast and musket ball artifacts. The trail led to 240 feet where artifacts were found, and then the bottom dropped out to the depths of over 300 feet. The depths were too great for divers. Only ROV's could go deeper.

The once-enthusiastic investors in Australia, however, refused to finance the next exploratory step, and the Pilar Project ended in disappointment. Nevertheless, with over 23,000 underwater hours logged in his dive book, Andy continued to travel worldwide as a master diver and salvage project manager.

In 2001 Kim Fisher asked Andy to return to the company as captain of the *M/V Magruder*. It was a welcome return to Key West. There was the *Atocha* sterncastle treasure yet to be found, and men with special skills and talents like Andy were needed in the vanguard of a new age of explorations. As captain of the *Magruder*, Andy both hires and trains the four divers in his crew.

"I love finding history underwater and seeing the expressions on the faces of the people who also find it. It is one of the greatest emotions ever, and I still get high off it."

Deep-water diving, however, has taken a toll on Andy's body. The accumulated water pressures have left him, at age 60, with hip and eye conditions that prevent him from diving deeper than 60 feet.

On Andy's home front, by 2014 his daughter Melissa had won a full scholarship and graduated from Yale University, and his high school senior son Andy was being acknowledged as a gifted video and filmmaker. Home for Andy and Monica was in Key West where the *Magruder* was docked. The only thing left for Andy to do as a career crown was to be present for the next great shipwreck treasure discovery. Whether it becomes the *Atocha* sterncastle, or the Lost Merchant, Andy Matroci deserves to be there.

The *Atocha* Mother Lode
Golden Crew Ring

THE DISCOVERY OF THE *Atocha* Mother Lode was an astounding event in July 1985, and everyone on the Fisher company team experienced a measure of fame and celebrity in the media frenzy that surrounded them. The treasure itself, however, was not available to be sold until after the Federal Court adjudication of Spring 1986 and the subsequent Division to company principals, expedition members, captains, crews, and the archaeological and administrative staff members. The reality in 1986 was that all the Division recipients were "treasure rich and money poor." It was not until 1987 when Mel Fisher himself received his first significant payment from the sale of silver coins that he was able to afford to make a heartfelt gift of gratitude to those whose endurance and dedication had made the *Atocha* quest a success. For them, Mel worked with Jostens to create the *Atocha* Mother Lode Golden Crew Ring.

Jostens, founded in 1887, is an American company providing yearbooks and class rings for high schools and colleges as well as championship rings for sports, including Super Bowl rings.

Each ring came with an Identification and Evaluation Certificate dated April 21, 1987, provided by Certified Gemological Sources. For Curtis White, crewmember of the *M/V Virgalona*, who received ring number 40, his custom created document read:

> "Gents #18 karat yellow gold (Diving Creations & Jostens special commission) "Atocha Golden Crew" commemorative ring. The heavy college style ring has sculptured sides with raised letters and numerals – "1622 (the year the Atocha sank), Treasure Salvors Inc." with carving depicting the Atocha – the other side – "1985" the year the Atocha was rediscovered) with carving depicting scuba diving equipment. The ring is set with one 13 mm x 11mm cushion shaped synthetic ruby (corundum) with diagonal white onyx stripe, serial #040, engraved Curtis W.E. White – each ring contains a portion of Atocha gold from the rediscovered wreck. (27.6 dwt). Approximate replacement value $1550."

The value of the Golden Crew rings over the years has obviously greatly increased, not only due to the price of gold, but also because these rings are the Super Bowl rings of the treasure salvage industry.

As you might expect from Mel's talent for showmanship, the unique rings were presented to the company veterans at a party held at the Ocean Key House. With each presentation, Mel and Deo handed the recipient a personal card. The front of the card that was presented with each individual ring was lettered "Nuestra Senora de Atocha Golden Crew, Ring #." The number of the ring was then hand lettered. Inside the card was the message, "In grateful appreciation of your devotion and hard work in the location and salvaging of the Atocha." The bottom of the card was signed "Deo Fisher" and "Mel Fisher."

The individuals who were given these Golden Crew rings are recognized today as members of a very exclusive society that intimately participated in one of the greatest exploration adventures in modern history.

Curtis White: Member of the *Atocha* Golden Crew

IF YOU WERE ONE of the 84 men and women who received an *Atocha* Golden Crew ring, you had stories to tell that could be appreciated only by each other. In his nine years of work with the Fisher salvage company from 1979 to 1988, Curtis William Erling White formed unique friendships and bonds with the principal actors in the greatest American treasure story ever told.

Curtis was on the deck of the M/V *Virgalona* when divers Andy Matroci and Greg Wareham popped to the surface and started screaming, "It's here! It's the main pile! We're sitting on silver bars."

"I heard the shouting, and I first thought that one of the divers was in trouble," Curtis remembers.

Curtis came to Key West, like many of the young adventurers of his generation, without a specific life direction. He had been raised in ports-of-call all over the world as the son of a Naval officer aviator and a culturally talented and refined mother. His formal upbringing, even in childhood, required him to wear a coat and tie. Curtis spent his high school years in Virginia Beach, Virginia, but his path as a young adult did not point to college or to a Naval career. Curtis had the "adventure gene," and he set out to explore his curiosity in various occupations. By the time he got to Key West in 1978, he had acquired a large set of construction and mechanical skills and so gained employment in an island boat yard. It was only a matter of time before he encountered Mel Fisher.

At age 26, physically strong, mentally alert, and highly skilled, Curtis was the right man for the jobs that Mel had in mind. Curtis would become the company builder, fabricator, troubleshooter, and repair swing-man for whatever Mel needed doing. He would be based on shore in a woodworking shop and serve in support of the boats, the museum, and even Mel's houseboats when necessary.

"I struck my own deal with Mel at a time when crewmembers on the boats were getting $50 a week and sleeping on the decks. I was getting a salary greater than what they were being paid, so it might have been a problem if I had not opened up my shop as their Key West party site. I have a gregarious personality.

You are my pal, and I trust you with my tools, and even with my girlfriends, until you give me a reason not to."

Before Curtis was certified to scuba dive in 1981, he had done construction jobs on the *Golden Doubloon* museum and office space, rebuilt Mel's houseboats, made repairs and refits on the salvage boats, built an aircraft camera mount for Pat Clyne and exhibits for shows in Washington, D.C. and New York City, and supported archaeologist Jim Sinclair by building fixtures in the conservation laboratory. Wherever a skilled craftsman was needed, Curtis was called.

Curtis also had another sideline where he could parlay his good looks, diving expertise, and cultural sophistication into income. He went on casting calls for national television commercials. In 1984 Curtis landed a role in the Miller High Life commercial titled "Charter Boat." This "Welcome to Miller Time" spot then played frequently during the telecast of the 1984 Olympic games, and months later, the residual payments kept coming until they totaled about $14,000. Income from doing commercials was especially welcome in the lean years when none of his fellow crewmembers had much pocket money. Curtis remembers the "hard times" parties as the best occasions for forming comradeship and brotherhood.

"We pooled our money together for rum and coke, fished for food, and provided our own entertainment. In our hearts, we thought that we lacked for nothing. I must admit, however, that sometimes those TV commercial residual checks arrived just in time to keep us going."

Years later, Curtis got feature film credits for *License to Kill* (1989) and for the video "Playboy: Sex on the Beach" (1997)

There is a certain level of celebrity that comes with the title of being a Mel Fisher treasure diver. Curtis White took the day off from duty on the *Virgalona* and was celebrating his birthday with his fiancée at an upscale restaurant when he was called to the phone. Who even knew where to locate him, he wondered. It was his roommate, Don Kincaid, telling him that 3,000 silver coins had been found that day and that he needed Curtis to help him recreate the find for the movie camera.

The next day, while Curtis worked underwater, guests in their own boats arrived on the site. When Curtis surfaced, one of the visitors extended his hand. To his surprise, the man offering his hand was Key West's most celebrated recording and performance star, Jimmy Buffett. Jimmy had been friends with Don Kincaid since the 1970s, and Don made the first-name introductions. Jimmy had been in the Keys shooting the cover for his 18th album, *Songs You Know by Heart*, which would be released in January 1985, to coincide with the opening of his Margaritaville store on Duval Street. The songs "Margaritaville" and "Changes in Latitude" had been huge hits in 1977. For the new album cover, Jimmy posed with his guitar in a beach hammock accompanied by two colorful parrots.

White and Kincaid always got front-row seats to Jimmy's New Year's Eve concerts in Key West, and they often encountered him at their favorite sushi bar. When Jimmy saw Curtis that December, he invited him to come to his home for a pre-concert dinner party. When Curtis entered the party, Jimmy began to introduce him as a "world famous treasure hunter." One of the guests was especially interested to hear Curtis tell his treasure stories, and he insisted that Curtis sit at his table for dinner.

The avid inquirer was a British man named Steve Winwood, the ultimate classic rock music star. Curtis recognized him immediately and knew well Winwood's hit songs "Valerie," "Back in the High Life Again," "Higher Love," and "Roll with It." Winwood, winner of two Grammy awards, was later inducted into the Rock and Roll Hall of Fame as the lead singer of the group Traffic. *Rolling Stone Magazine* named Steve Winwood number 33 on its list of 100 Greatest Singers of All Time.

But there was yet another future member of the Rock and Roll Hall of Fame (2000) at the party. It was James Taylor, a five-time Grammy award winner whose 1970s mega hits "Fire and Rain" and "You've Got a Friend" made him a folk rock, blues, and country music legend. His 1976 *Greatest Hits* album sold more than 12 million copies. To these pals of Jimmy Buffett who were show business superstars, the other celebrities at the party were the Key West treasure hunters. It was a night that Curtis would never forget.

Prior to the *Atocha* Mother Lode being discovered, there were about 35 Fisher company employees. During the 1985-87 excavation of the underwater site, the employee roster jumped to 84. Even those who had worked only the recovery period received the Golden Crew rings.

After his years with the Fisher company, Curtis stayed in Key West as a permanent resident and acquired a 100-ton Master's License with auxiliary endorsements for Sail and Towing. He also obtained certification as a scuba dive supervisor and completed thousands of dives on both American coasts and the Caribbean. His working title is Captain Curtis White by virtue of having operated a 53-foot catamaran out of Key West for 13 years for owner Don Kincaid. Meanwhile, Curtis took a real estate course and became a licensed Florida realtor. His specialty, of course, is Key West properties.

The outrageously adventurous men and women who gave the youth of their twenties and early thirties to the *Atocha* quest are now embracing their sixties. Small groups of them still stage informal annual meetings to recall their days of glory. Others keep track of each other on Facebook and by e-mail. A trip up or down the Keys may include a drop-in for coffee or a meal that sustains the friendships. Names among the 84 ring wearers come up, and their stories are retold—stories that do not appear in any books or any films, stories that exist only for those who experienced them.

36

Don Kincaid: Adventurer
with a Camera

ASIDE FROM FISHER FAMILY members, Dr. Gene Lyon, Fay Field, Duncan Mathewson, Pat Clyne, and Bleth McHaley, perhaps the most mentioned name in the *Atocha* story literature is Don Kincaid.

Don's childhood included fishing, boating, and snorkeling in the waters off Key West where he developed a personal fascination for ocean life and shipwrecks. As a nine-year-old on a military transport ship to join his Air Force sergeant father in the Philippines, Don passed through the many WWII sunken ships still clogging Manila Bay. The idea of being able to dive on a sunken ship possessed him, and Don began to haunt the post library in search of anything about shipwreck diving. Then his father gave him two issues of *Water World Magazine*. One of the magazine features was about a California man who was diving for gold nuggets in the same rivers that the '49ers had worked.

The man was Mel Fisher, and across from the article was a small advertisement for Mel's Aqua Shop, the first scuba dive shop in the USA.

Don had to have been a precocious high school teenager while living in the Hampton, Virginia area when he took an interest in Civil War shipwrecks. Don and his diving buddies then found and dove on half a dozen wrecks on the Pamunkey River below Richmond and recovered artifacts that he shared with

the Mariner's Museum in Newport News, now designated by Congress as America's National Maritime Museum. Union General George McClellan established a supply depot on the Pamunkey River to support the largest combined land and water military force ever assembled. The objective was Richmond, the Confederate capital; and in the spring of 1862, the Confederates scuttled over 60 schooners and steamers in the river in an attempt to delay McClellan's advance. The Union campaign stalled in July 1862, and the Confederate shipwrecks languished in archaeological obscurity for over 100 years.

The young explorer began to spend a lot of his free time in the Mariner's Museum huge library that was devoted to the sea.

Librarian John Lockhead then became his guide to the classics of shipwreck history, and he began to mentor Don in the archaeology and conservation of shipwreck artifacts.

As Don became more involved in underwater photography, he realized that he would need formal training to become a professional. His best option was to join the regular Army that promised him the military occupation specialty of his choice. He began basic training in September of 1966, and six weeks later he was sent to the Army's film school at Ft. Monmouth, New Jersey. His first assignment was at the Army Pictorial Center in New York City where he served as an assistant cameraman on both 16 mm and 35 mm film productions and learned the craft of makeup, lighting, and special effects. Then sent to Germany as a still photographer, he used his pass and leave days to follow and photograph the Grand Prix motorsport racing circuit all over Europe.

Out of the Army in 1969, Don returned to New York City to work several jobs in photo labs and studios while contributing photos as a stringer for *Auto Racing Magazine*. He also took classes in photojournalism and underwater photography. But for Don, home was Key West, and the Florida Keys were where he could make a career as an underwater photographer, maybe even a shipwreck photographer.

Although Don was overqualified to work in Conn's Camera in Key West, the part-time job allowed him to hitch rides on dive boats and begin to assemble a portfolio of underwater photographs. Don had been working behind the camera store counter about a month when a couple came in for the quick repair of a 16 mm film projector. They looked vaguely familiar to Don, but he did not make the connection until the man paid with a Treasure Salvors, Inc. check and signed it "Mel Fisher."

There, face-to-face, were the man and his beautiful redheaded diver wife that Don had followed in various publications since his childhood.

The timing of the unexpected encounter could not have been better for both parties. Mel was also an underwater photographer and filmmaker; but due to the pressures of operating a salvage company both on land and sea, and the constant need to obtain expedition member support, Mel was no longer available to chronicle his own adventures.

"Well, Mr. Fisher," the lanky, bespeckled 25-year-old said, "I am a trained filmmaker, photojournalist, and diver. I have worked on Civil War wrecks, and I have some training in archaeology. Do you need someone to shoot a story on your treasure hunt?"

At first, Don began photographing Mel's operations on weekends and whenever he could string a few days off from the camera shop. Then on May 1, 1971, Don became a full-time employee at $60 a week. By the 11th, on his 26th birthday, only five months after leaving New York, Don was in the Marquesas Keys diving off Bob Holloway's 34-foot Chris Craft *Holly's Folly*.

"I was now a fulltime treasure diving photographer," Don said. "Quite possibly, I was the only person on the planet with that job description."

Don worked alternately between *Holly's Folly*, which towed the magnetometer and the *Virgalona*, the company's dive boat equipped with the mailboxes. About this period, Don has written:

> "Treasure hunting is a lot of hard work. It is also wet, cold, hot, uncomfortable, boring, and inherently dangerous. Usually all of the above at about the same time. We worked from dawn til after dark, or until something broke, or until we ran out of fuel and food."

One of Don's first highlights on the *Virgalona* was to photograph the discovery of a large Spanish galleon anchor. A few days later, Don was diving in a big clear-water crater that had been hollowed out by the *Virgalona's* mailboxes when something bright caught his eye. When he pulled the object out of the sand, it proved to be a chain 8 1/2 feet long with links 3/8" in diameter. Kincaid thought that it looked like brass; but as he approached the sunlit surface, he says, the chain started getting "brighter and brighter." On deck, it was immediately recognized as gold.

The discovery was an emotional moment. Deo hugged Don, and Mel wept. As the first piece of gold recovered from the *Atocha*, Kincaid made history. Mel valued the chain at over $120,000 and rewarded his diver/photographer with a gold coin. Don still wears it. Everybody on the salvage boats wanted to be photographed with the gold chain draped around their neck, and gold fever swept over everyone in the company. Mel was then quick to file salvage permits from the State of Florida.

Don Kincaid seemed to have a destiny for being present at the most dramatic events in the Fishers' search for the *Atocha*. Don was there to photograph the recovery of a chest load of sulfided silver pieces-of-eight for archaeological identification. Once Don thought that he was caught alone on a crew houseboat within the Marquesas Key when a hurricane was approaching. But a crew boat and a tour boat had departed missing one passenger. A young woman tour guide from the *Golden Doubloon* had taken a walk on the beach and missed her connection. Don found her and took her aboard the houseboat. Together they rode out the storm and saved the houseboat by putting out all anchors and tying the bow to the mangroves.

When Kim Fisher's boat recovered three silver bars with identifying marks under their encrustation, Don, along with a

National Geographic Society photographer, rushed to the scene to document the incredible moment when Gene Lyon matched the numbers on the silver bars to the *Atocha* manifest. When Dirk Fisher on the *Northwind* discovered five bronze cannons from the *Atocha* in July 1975, Don went with Duncan Mathewson to photograph the cannons in situ and to map and photograph the site. During their work underwater, four additional bronze cannons were found, for a total of nine.

By the end of the week, the team had completed mapping and photographing, so two of the eight-foot-long cannons were hoisted onboard the *Northwind*. One of the cannons was marked with its weight of 3,110 pounds, and Duncan Mathewson was able to confirm from a list of the *Atocha*'s cannons the significance of the discovery. With all these heavy cannons in the same area, the salvors expected the *Atocha* Mother Lode to be close at hand. A jubilant Mel Fisher returned to Key West to show off the *Atocha* cannons to a waiting worldwide press corps.

During the years that Don Kincaid was associated with the searches, discoveries, and recoveries of the *Atocha* and *Santa Margarita* treasures, he was often in the employ of the National Geographic Society who wanted a proven professional underwater photographer on site to document the Fisher salvage activities. In the late fall and winter off-season, Don reverted to employment by the Fisher company to work on their special projects. Many company exhibits and promotional materials include Don's photos and films. Don was also qualified to captain a large salvage boat, and he was often at the helm of the *Virgalona* when needed. Mel had a special fondness for people who had both multiple skill sets plus the capacity to get things done.

The great achievement of finding and identifying the *Atocha* bronze cannons was too soon to be overshadowed by a great personal tragedy, and Don Kincaid would be the intimate witness of it all. Dirk Fisher's boat, the *Northwind*, had returned to Key West to both celebrate and provision. Then, anxious to get back on the trail of the *Atocha*, the *Northwind* returned to the salvage site on Sunday, July 19th. Don was on board to photograph the expected finds of the next day.

The crew had brought along baskets of fried chicken so that Angel Fisher, Dirk's wife, would not have to cook supper on her birthday. There was a quiet birthday party, and then the crew settled in to get needed sleep in preparation for the Monday salvage day. The accounts of the capsizing of the *Northwind* in the early dark hours of the 20th are numerous, but all of them describe Don Kincaid as the first person to awake to the boat's alarming list and his attempts to alert the others on the boat. Of the 11 on board, three—Dirk and Angel Fisher and diver Rick Gage—were trapped in their cabins and perished. The survivors, adrift and clinging to a makeshift life raft, were rescued after sunrise by the crew of the *Virgalona*. Don, still in the water, was the one who told Kim Fisher above him on the boat deck that Kim's brother and the others were lost. Don remembers that Kim nearly collapsed with shock and grief, and that he went to his cabin in total despair.

Don was back in the water with the other divers later for the recovery of the bodies. It was a solemn, dreadful duty. Out of respect, the bodies were wrapped in sheets before they were brought to the surface. The same day, Don dove on the *Northwind* again to recover his camera gear and equipment belonging to National Geographic.

Six months later, National Geographic assigned him to dive on the *Northwind* to film it for their archives. It was emotionally difficult for Don to swim in and around the sunken vessel.

In one scene Don filmed his hand reaching through a porthole to recover a coffee cup still hanging from its hook in the galley. When he showed the footage to a National Geographic staff audience in Washington, the unexpected hand caused an immediate gasp reaction. The footage thus far has never been shown to the public.

After the great tragedy of July 1975, it was emotionally difficult to return to the treasure hunt, but each person who knew Dirk understood that he, of all people, would want them to continue. There were productive and non-treasure-producing years throughout the late 1970s; and then in February 1980, very early in the search season, the *Santa Margarita* was found. By the end of that summer, Don Kincaid had filmed the recovery of a significant treasure recovered from the *Santa Margarita*. The 54 gold bars and disks alone weighed 106 pounds. There were also 43 gold chains, 53 gold coins, and nearly 12,000 silver coins. This discovery stimulated investor confidence. Two major capital investment firms based in New York and New Jersey then entered the financial picture, and they raised over $10 million to underwrite Treasure Salvors, Inc. Finally, the Fisher company had the means and the resources to mount an aggressive quest for the *Atocha*.

In the February 1982 issue of *National Geographic Magazine*, Don's text and photos were featured in an article about the salvaging of the *Santa Margarita*. It was a touchstone professional credit in his career.

Don Kincaid remained a key company leader and documentarian throughout the ten years of financial and emotional challenges that spanned the gulf between the *Northwind* tragedy of July 20, 1975, and the finding of the *Atocha* Mother Lode on July 20,

1985. Those, like Don, who had been intimately involved with both events, were struck hard by its mystifying synchronicity.

During the recovery of the *Atocha* Mother Lode, Don again filmed underwater for *National Geographic*. In 1986 he authored a *National Geographic* feature story on the Mother Lode with his own photos. It would have been another major league photojournalism credit, but the article got pulled when the National Geographic television feature documentary ellipsed it. It seemed to Don that the film and magazine departments at the National Geographic were in competition with each other. Nevertheless, Don's film footage and still photos remain accessible in the National Geographic archives, and he earns occasional fees from their use.

In the 1986 television movie *Dreams of Gold: The Mel Fisher Story*, where Mel is played by Cliff Robertson and Deo by Loretta Swit, the role of Don Kincaid is played by Scott Paulin. Paulin, who appeared in *The Right Stuff* (1983), got fourth billing in the Fisher story movie. He later earned feature credits in *Turner & Hooch* (1989) and *I Am Sam* (2001) and has appeared on many dramatic television series. In a trivia note, the part of Kim Fisher was played by William Zabka, who will be remembered as the mean blonde adversary of *The Karate Kid* (1984).

When the *Atocha* Golden Crew Rings were handed out in 1987, Don was presented with ring number 17. With his share of the *Atocha* Mother Lode treasure, Don retreated to residence on a sailboat out of the Key West celebrity limelight. Then he went to work on his idea of a catamaran sailboat large enough to conduct history and ecology snorkel tours. From 1971, when Don began going to sea with Treasure Salvors, Inc., to 2006, when he quit his catamaran, he averaged 208 days a year on the water. Don was the captain of record for *The Stars & Stripes* sailing catamaran and worked the boat several days a week. Two of his

Fisher company pals, Curtis White and Bruce Etschman, also worked the boat as captains.

"The thing about former Treasure Salvors, Inc. divers that I worked with, is that they have far more experience at sea than most charter boat captains," Don says. "I know that they will always do the right things to keep their passengers safe."

The enjoyment of giving passengers the thrill of catamaran sailing through the Keys lasted for 16 years between 1990 and 2006. Hurricanes in 2004 and 2005, however, caused forced evacuations and the loss of business days that could not be recovered. The tour operation ended.

Don was a board member of Treasure Salvors, Inc. and company vice president from the late 1970s. He also served terms on the board of directors of the Mel Fisher Maritime Museum. Since 1998, he has served on the Advisory Council for the Florida Keys National Marine Sanctuary.

Don has his *Atocha* Golden Crew ring to show, but he also has a one-of-a-kind tie tack made from the ring design. "Not that I own any ties," he says. The tie tack was given to Don by Mel in the year before the rings were made and presented. If you are lucky enough to catch someone wearing a Golden Crew ring, and you can convince them to chat over a meal or other libation as your guest, you may well open up a treasure chest of stories that can only be told by the individuals who lived them. You will then discover that the stories and the people of the *Atocha* Golden Crew ring are very unique. They are true modern American pioneers.

37

How to Join Kim and Lee

IT IS NO SECRET, if you talk to the right people who have an affinity for the romance of Key West, that you can join the most successful treasure hunting salvage company in the world. Maybe you have seen the multiple National Geographic documentary films or read the extensive articles and books about Mel Fisher's Treasures and experienced the vicarious thrill of imagining yourself on a scuba dive where you actually lay hands on a silver piece-of-eight, a gold doubloon or gold chain, or a rosary studded with emeralds, that has defied the sands of time since 1622.

It is a fact that about 70% of the members in any given salvage season renew their contracts with Mel Fisher's Expeditions. They renew for a variety of good reasons. First, members renew at the same rate of their original buy-in. For example, in the year 2000, a Class A membership cost $50,000. It was $60,000 in 2001 to 2004; $72,000 in 2005; $80,000 in 2006 to 2011, and $100,000 from 2012 to 2014. Partial memberships are in one-eighth increments; i.e., $12,500 in 2014. A 2000 Class A member is still able to acquire a 1% interest in the division of treasure for a new salvage season for the same $50,000 cost while a first-time Class A member in 2014 must pay $100,000.

The second, and perhaps the most coveted benefit of expedition membership, is that members may dive on the *Atocha* salvage sites many times and enjoy company hospitality and services year after year. They become part of the Key West culture through their long association with the Fisher family. The staff at Investor Relations knows their members by name and is willing to provide concierge services for visits to Key West throughout the year.

Need a hotel room? Want to go fishing? As an expedition member, you are treated as a VIP by Mel Fisher's Expeditions whether you come to town to dive on their treasure sites or just to enjoy the weather and excitement of Florida's island playground paradise. Then, of course, there is Division Week, an annual extravagant week of diving, parties, and fun where you receive your share of the *Atocha* treasure that was salvaged during your membership year. A description of Division Week can be seen on the website www.melfisher.com.

Since treasure-salvaging seasons are historically uneven, potential members are advised in extensive detail about the difficulties of finding artifacts of great value. A large binder holds the Confidential Private Placement Memorandum (PPM). To call it a full disclosure document would be an understatement of what it contains. The PPM establishing Mel Fisher Expedition – 2014 LLC covered expeditions to recover artifacts from the *Atocha*, the *Margarita*, and the Lost Merchant Shipwreck Project. The documentation covers every procedure and condition as both a complete briefing and a disclaimer. Class A memberships in the Expedition are not registered securities and cannot be resold or transferred. Then, too, because the PPM details every aspect of the Mel Fisher's Expeditions' operations, the offering document is confidential.

Of special interest to most first-time expedition members is information on exactly how their share of annual treasure is calculated. All recovered artifacts are logged, appraised, certified, and assigned a point value. The point criteria is based on past prices through sales of similar items, opinions of appraisers and other historic shipwreck artifact experts, and values accepted by the IRS in connection with donations of similar items. Depending on the size of the membership interest the member has, the total number of points due to each member is calculated. Member accounts are then assigned a code, and a computer program generates a distribution by the random selection of artifacts by point value. The blind, double-random selection process is thus accomplished without bias, and impartiality is assured.

In the old days, a guy in a bar might show you a treasure map and offer you riches if you could only finance a boat and crew to bring the treasure home. There might be a contract on a bar napkin. Maybe it takes the same imagination to take a chance on treasure hunting today. But if you are so inclined, you'd be better to trust the professional with the disclosure documents over the guy with the faded map and wet bar napkin.

Documenting Treasure Artifacts

R. Duncan Mathewson, shipwreck archaeologist

As R. Duncan Mathewson III, past Archaeological Director of Mel Fisher's Treasure Salvors, Inc., has said, "the real purpose of archaeology is to enable scholars to reconstruct the fine detail of history and increase our understanding of life in the past." When centuries-old historic sites like the *Atocha* and the *Santa Margarita* are discovered in seawater, the task to recover, document, conserve, and curate its artifacts is a long professionally demanding process.

Duncan Mathewson's first introduction to the Key West treasure hunters was at the 1972 annual meeting of the Florida Historical Society where he met Dr. Gene Lyon, the Spanish colonial era historian who was already a key member of the Fisher company team. Although Duncan, an American graduate of Dartmouth College, had completed four years of graduate studies toward his Ph.D. in archaeology at universities in Edinburgh, Scotland and London, England, and had done field work in West Africa and in Jamaica, his incompleted non-American Ph.D. was a barrier to employment in his own country.

Duncan and Gene became peer correspondents as Duncan continued work with materials salvaged from Port Royal, the Jamaican pirate capital that had sunk into Kingston Harbor during an earthquake in 1692. This connection to Spanish colonial archaeology led Gene to recommend Duncan to Mel, and in June 1973, Mel had sent him a telegram and a plane ticket as an invitation to come to Key West.

When Mel employed Duncan in early July 1973, marine archaeology was a very young science, and the few academics in the field were new to scuba diving and unwilling to be associated with treasure hunters. Duncan arrived in Key West on the same exciting day 60-pound silver ingots that bore the tally numbers that appeared on the *Atocha* manifest were brought to port. It seemed like proof positive that Mel was justified in his claims for the *Atocha*, but bitter salvage competitors, and even state officials, challenged their authenticity.

Mathewson witnessed first hand the controversy surrounding the silver ingots recovery, and he recognized that good archaeology was needed to establish Mel's claims to the *Atocha*. He saw it as the archaeological challenge of a lifetime, and so despite no diving experiences or marine site training, Mathewson cast his professional career lot with the salvors. He soon set many prec-edents for the future of marine archaeology, and ultimately, he became one of the most successful scientists in his field.

Underwater or marine archaeology initially struggled to establish its scientific bona fides due to the pirate reputations of some shipwreck salvagers. It was only in the late 1980s that the field of maritime archaeology was recognized as an academic discipline that was taught at universities. Marine archaeology, however, is not restricted to the study of shipwrecks. It includes the historic remains of bridges and harbors, for example, that lie underwater. Investigating an underwater site requires a great deal more logistics than working land sites. Support vessels and certified divers also greatly increase the expense of operations.

When a shipwreck is scattered over miles of ocean bottom and hidden under sands deposited by centuries of storms, the mosaic picture of its people and their culture is very difficult to reconstruct. It must be assembled item by item and interpreted by experts in fields as diverse as ship construction and numismat-ics. The *Atocha* shipwreck is a time capsule that contains the essen-tials of how a world-dominating culture lived in the year 1622.

Today, the use of DGPS (differential global positioning system) technology is the key to accurate positioning, which is a basic requirement for this type of work. Next, a topographi-cal survey and a site plan showing the location of the artifacts and related materials are needed. Divers must carry out a three-dimensional survey using depth gauges and tape measures. ROV's may be employed for these tasks in extreme depths.

The underwater discoveries must be recorded in situ. Scale drawing using special pencils that write on plastic dive slates, digital still and video cameras adapted for use underwater are the major recording tools that obviously require trained and talented operators. Excavation of the underwater archaeology site requires additional skill sets as silt and sediments are removed by a venturi dredge or airlift to expose the varied artifacts that range from a huge anchor to a single gold toothpick.

The archaeological methods of 1985 that were employed to document the *Atocha* have been greatly enhanced by technological developments as exemplified by the *Dolores*. With her survey, positioning, and photographic capabilities, *Dolores* can document a salvage site in a fraction of the time that a crew of divers trained in archaeology could accomplish the same task.

Artifacts, especially metal ones, that are recovered from seawater need stabilization to counteract the absorption of salt that leads to corrosion. This conservation process needs to begin as soon as the objects arrive on deck. Conservation of shipwreck artifacts is both time consuming and expensive. Without conservation, however, many artifacts will deteriorate at a very rapid rate and lose their archaeological value.Organic material like leather, wood, textile, and rope, for example, can crumble into dust within hours of being taken out of seawater unless treated by a trained conservator. Even iron, bone, glazed ceramics, and pottery will eventually deteriorate if not properly conserved. The purpose of conservation is to document, analyze, clean, and stabilize an object of historic or cultural interest. Restoration of an artifact may be desirable, but the primary concern is always conservation. The basic data collected when the artifact is first discovered stays with it as an informational chain link that is essential to its curation. Today, "Methods of Conserving Archaeological Material from Underwater Sites" is a university course of study that is complemented by a Conservation Manual that has been published since 1996 in updated revisions.

To provide appreciation for a single silver coin from the *Atocha*, for example, the archaeologist and the historian would be provided with a huge volume of information. The preamble to the artifact identification begins with the archival research that tells the background story of the ship itself and details of its loss at sea. Then follows an account of the relentless search by the treasure salvors whose dreams and passions carry it from mythology to the realms of Hollywood dramas. In the focus on the *Atocha*, the drama is about real boats, captains, crews, and divers at risk who actually discover huge treasures and bring them up from the ocean bottom to be displayed on the decks of their victorious salvage vessels. If the treasure hunters were amateurs in the field, the tale that they tell would end there, but for professionals like Mel Fisher's Treasure Salvors, Inc., the discovery of any shipwreck artifact is just the beginning of their obligation to record and preserve the evidence of past lifestyles that are of cultural importance.

Every step of the information process is critical to the later interpretation of a recovered artifact. What was its attitude on the shipwreck site? What objects were found near it? These two questions alone require underwater site drawings, logs, photographs, measurements, and artist sketches. Conservation and curation begins at this point as each artifact is described and catalogued for later cross-referencing.

The recovery of more than 250,000 artifacts from the *Atocha* and *Santa Margarita* has added greatly to a cultural understanding of the Spanish colonial Americas. For the archaeology community, the pottery, plates, weapons, navigational instruments, hull spikes, and the everyday personal items carried by soldiers, sailors, priests, and passengers are as valued as the silver, gold, and jewels that spilled from the treasure chests.

Kim sums up the Fisher family's contribution to marine archaeology.

"When my Dad first started recovering historic shipwreck material, Florida had no bureaucracy set up to handle the situation. Under a contract with our company Real Eight, the State received twenty-five percent of all recoveries. I remember one of the first divisions where the State sent a state trooper to Vero Beach, and we made four piles of silver coins of equal weight. The trooper picked one, and we then loaded that pile into his trunk. The gold coins and other more valuable items, of course, received a lot more attention.

"My dad realized early on the importance of proper archaeology. First, by recording all the information possible about each artifact, it preserved all that information for future generations. Second, by recording where each item was found, we could develop a scatter pattern or "trail" and know where we were most likely to find more artifacts. Last, but not least, by creating an unbroken chain of authenticity starting on the day an item is recovered, we enhance the value of each item.

"Through the years we developed a set of rules or "archaeological guidelines" which were adopted by the State of Florida and later by the Florida Keys National Marine Sanctuary. These guidelines have also been adopted by numerous other countries. Every once in a while, the guidelines are modified with the advent of new technology. For example, when DGPS satellite navigation became accurate enough, the guidelines were adapted to allow its use since it is the most accurate system available."

39

Jim Sinclair: Primary Archaeologist

THE CURRENT PRIMARY ARCHAEOLOGIST and artifact investigator for the Fisher company is a veteran of the late 1970s when the search for the *Atocha* was at its peak. In 1978 Jim Sinclair was a junior at the prestigious Franklin Pierce College, a small, private institution in Rindge, New Hampshire. He was near graduating with a BA degree in anthropology, and he was already wondering what his job prospects would be in that narrow field.

Pierce College encouraged its students to leave campus during a January break in the academic schedule to explore personal interests with a credit incentive. Jim Sinclair reviewed his options and happened on Sea Camp, a program conducted by The Newfound Harbor Marine Institute as an introduction to underwater archaeology. As an anthropology major, marine archaeology was close enough to earn the January credit, so Jim negotiated family financial support and left the winter of New Hampshire for the warm, sunny environment of Big Pine Key, Florida, only 30 miles north of Key West.

For college young people, Sea Camp must have seemed like a fantasy come true. The accommodations were dormitory, but there were equal numbers of males and females for bathing suit encounters in the dining area, the recreation hall, the classrooms and science labs, and also during water sports like scuba, sailing, and windsurfing. What was not to love about marine science?

The host and programmer for the ten-day Sea Camp event was none other than Duncan Mathewson, the archaeological director of the search for the *Atocha*, aided by veteran under-

water photographer Don Kincaid, who had documented the Fisher company's treasure hunt since 1971. Both were key members of the Mel Fisher team, so who should they feature for the finale of the Sea Camp adventure but the great explorer himself, Mel Fisher.

Mel showed a National Geographic documentary film about his exploits and then talked for hours as the academic gathering transitioned into the camaraderie of a memorable party. At the end of the night, Mel extended an open invitation to the college participants. Jim remembers him saying, "When you graduate, come on down to Key West and help me hunt for treasure." Jim took Mel's words as a job offer.

Jim's first job with the Fisher organization was to expand the conservation laboratory in Key West. Duncan Mathewson had begun as a one-man operation; but as the volume of artifacts greatly increased, he had to expand his archaeological staff and also train the ship captains and divers in recovery and documentation procedures. By the summer of 1985, the archaeological staff grew to 15, with another 20 outside scholars involved with identifying the *Atocha* artifacts. Jim Sinclair was then in charge of the conservation staff that continued to process the thousands of *Atocha* artifacts that were being salvaged. As an employee of the Fisher company, Jim assisted with developing conservation techniques and archaeological guidelines that are still in practice today—30 years later. Jim went on to maximize his on-the-job experiences with the Fisher company by earning a master's degree in Maritime Historic Archaeology from the Union Institute and University.

After the *Atocha* Mother Lode was found in 1985, Jim received a team member's share in the 1986 great Division year, and he continued to work for the Fisher company and assist The Mel Fisher Maritime Heritage Society that was preparing artifacts for museum display.

Years later, Jim and his wife Lisa, and their sales team, hit the road five days a week for 38 weeks a year. Jim, as the archaeologist, opened the sale sessions with a 45-minute introductory talk that detailed the historical background of the *Atocha*, its sinking, and the great exploration that had led to its recovery. On the road, he was obligated to give the talk three to five times a day! This activity is not the kind of thing that qualifies you for membership in The Explorers Club.

The Explorers Club was founded in New York City in 1904 to promote scientific exploration of land, sea, air, and space by supporting pioneer research and education. There are only about 3,000 members of the club scattered over more than 60 countries in 26 chapters around the world. These clubrooms are like those pictured in the adventure movies where legendary explorers meet, bond, and plan to astound the world with their exploits. Explorers Club members have been responsible for an illustrious series of famous firsts: first to the North and South Poles, first to the summit of Mount Everest, first to the deepest point in the ocean, and first to the surface of the moon. Jim Sinclair earned his place in the Explorers Club in 2000 and 2001 in a Russian MIR, a self-propelled deep submergence vehicle. MIR, by the way, is the Russian word for "peace."

Jim was the first professional archaeologist to visit the wreck site of the RMS *Titanic* using a MIR. He performed the first archaeological survey of the stern artifact-scattered sediment field. The following year, he was the lead archaeologist on a MIR dive to a historic-period shipwreck that had been discovered at 16,300 feet in the Blake Basin of the mid-Atlantic. At the time (2001), it was the deepest archaeological ship recovery in history. The wreckage seemed English, and its cargo of rum bottles and coconuts prompted it to be named the *"Piña Colada."* The descent to 16,300 feet in a MIR requires 3 1/2 hours. The ascent, due to the build-up of pressure, takes even longer—5 hours.

Among the artifacts recovered from the *Piña Colada* was a gold box with 14 gold coins wrapped in a piece of newspaper. The newsprint was still legible, and it contained an article that dated an event to 1810. The recovered stoneware, flintlock pistols with brass barrels, octants, a wooden telescope, and 1300 silver coins were among the artifacts that dated the wreck to before 1812.

Today, Jim Sinclair is a founding member and current board member of the Professional Marine Explorers Society. He

resides in St. Augustine, Florida, the oldest continuously occupied European-established settlement and port in the continental United States. Founded in 1565, years prior to the wreck of
the *Atocha*, St. Augustine served as the capital of Spanish Florida
for over 200 years. For Spanish colonial historian Dr. Eugene
Lyon, who found the *Atocha* manifests in the archives of Spain,
and Jim Sinclair, who archaeologically interpreted its artifacts,
old St. Augustine is as close as scholars can get in America to
the Spanish colonial empire. It must be very stimulating to walk
those historical streets with their background.

40

Follow the Coin

FOR THE SAKE OF becoming an insider to the real work of professional shipwreck salvors, let's follow the process of a single silver eight reale coin, a "piece-of-eight," from its moment of recovery from the *Atocha* wreck site to its place as a "one of a kind" piece of jewelry registered into the World's Most Famous Treasure Collection. It is the iconic necklace of Key West, a piece-of-eight mounted and worn proudly by all who know the story of their hometown legend Mel Fisher. You may hear the locals fondly refer to it as their "Key West dog tag."

Let's begin with the discovery and recovery process. On the day the *Atocha* Mother Lode was found, Andy Matroci was one of the first divers on the treasure. Archaeologist Duncan Mathewson quickly recognized Andy also as a "reliable archaeological recorder" and a principal compiler of the artifact inventory. While other divers celebrated on deck, Andy and Duncan assigned individual tag numbers to each artifact and entered them into the ship's log. Duncan also interviewed Andy for details of what he had seen on the bottom. The huge stack of silver ingots that Andy had discovered left no question in Duncan's mind that they had found the *Atocha* Mother Lode, but there had to be scientific confirmation before such claims could be made. Little did they know their documentation and management of the wreck itself would become the precursor for the State of Florida guidelines on underwater shipwreck archaeology. Critics abounded on both sides of the question of whether commercial salvage and marine archaeology could co-exist.

Today, however, with the Mel Fisher Maritime Museum in evidence on land, a complete archaeological History of the *Atocha* intact, and standard operating procedures for marine archaeology being practiced at sea, the Fisher company has well proven it can be done. From the CEO of the Mel Fisher company Kim Fisher through the chain of executives, department managers, boat captains and crews, all are well aware of their responsibilities to preserve the historic value of their maritime history through archaeological documentation along with their efforts in salvaging underwater shipwrecks.

A seasoned salvor knows the value of recording the archaeological information as it tells a story which leads to a larger picture for the site, through details of the scatter pattern. With the wreck properly documented, the salvor can then get a better picture of the artifact trail and logically plot a direction for the remains of the wreck. Archaeological data thus saves time and the expense when considering equipment, crews, weather, and the fuel costs of a salvage operation.

The direction that a shipwreck anchor is pointing, for example, indicates to the salvor the direction of the currents at the time of the sinking. The attitudes of artifacts and the extension of an imaginary anchor line by compass degrees indicate the direction of the ship. Noting the cargo patterns on the ocean floor, paying close attention to their locations in situ, and knowing heavy material will settle into the bottom sediments faster than lighter artifacts helps to determine the beginning of the trail. Potentially the location of lighter material will disclose the direction to follow for a continued scatter pattern of artifacts. The *Atocha* trail to date is nine miles long.

This is now a 30-year process since the discovery of the *Atocha's* Mother Lode in 1985. The Mel Fisher company officials continue to use the resources of archaeology to determine where to look next. They continue to document every hole where they have moved the sand to search and every artifact ever recovered on site prior to arriving at the lab. They thus have created an unbroken chain of authenticity required to register each artifact into the *Atocha* Collection.

"In the early days," Andy recalls, "we cut a fifty-five-gallon steel drum longways to make an on-deck freshwater tank. We set the tanks in a wooden frame and covered them with a wooden top. In photos of the *Dauntless*, you can see the artifact tanks on the deck. It was crude, but it worked."

Duncan Mathewson did not want any artifacts brought up from the bottom to remain too long in the open air. For captains today, the protocol is to meet a diver at the dive ladder and take possession of any artifact brought onboard. If an artifact is too large or heavy to be brought up by hand, a plan is initiated to recover it. Fragile objects are always given special attention. After surviving 350 years intact on the bottom of the ocean, great care is taken to protect each artifact in its first moments of recovery.

The basic procedure for processing an artifact has not changed much since it was instituted in the 1980s. The captain tags each item with an assigned tag number and writes a brief description of what he thinks it is. Each single coin, for example, gets a separate tag number. A clump of coins fused together would be assigned one tag number until they are separated in the conservation lab and sent on to Curating to receive their individual ID number. The Artifact Recovery form is in triplicate. One copy will stay with the captain, one copy will go with the artifact to the lab, and one copy goes to the Curating Department. An electronic copy is sent to the Florida Keys National Marine Sanctuary.

The boat captain turns the artifacts over to the company conservator who then verifies each item on the list. Once conservation is completed in the lab, the artifact will go to Curating where it will be photographed, weighed, measured, given a registration/ID number, and entered into the data banks. Then it goes into a safe until adjudication of title has been completed. From there the piece may go out to an expedition member, or be donated to the museum, or go for sale in one of the gift shops. Here is where the public can actually "Own a Piece of History."

41

From Conservation to Sale

FROM THE SEA TO the lab, your potential piece-of-eight is now entrusted to the care of John Corcoran, the company's chief conservator, who maintains a secure laboratory on the fourth floor of the 200 Greene Street building. John is a quietly intense department manager who joined the company in Mel Fisher's last year.

For more than 15 years, John has accumulated a great deal of expertise in the conservation of shipwreck artifacts. He remembers a Spanish nobleman's dagger as being the most difficult object to conserve. The dagger presented four different metals—iron, steel, gold, and silver—plus a rare wood handle to conserve. The dagger remained submerged in the electrolytic reduction tank for a year, except for the twenty minutes a day that John needed to remove the layers of encrustations with small dental pick-type tools.

An iron cannon weighing in excess of a thousand pounds required several years in the electrolytic reduction tanks for the removal of its marine salts. It was his heaviest project. The most expensive artifact that John personally conserved was a gold chalice valued at over a million dollars. Another challenging artifact that he remembers well was a gold rosary cross with wooden beads. A piece of wood at the center of the gold cross was possibly

John Corcoran, chief conservator, works with an artifact in an electrolytic reduction tank.

a fake relic reputed to be from the Christian crucifixion cross, or maybe it is from the cross on which Christ was crucified. John delights in doing his own artifact research and including those observations in the official database. The wooden elements of the rosary had added six months to the conservation process.

The company policy is not to interrupt John's work in the lab except for pre-scheduled tours by the company's financial supporters. Invited into the lab's large space, one is first struck by the eight electrolytic reduction tanks that measure three feet in width, eight feet in length, and two feet in depth. Looking over the side of any one of the tanks is a look into nautical history. There you may see pieces-of-eight dating from 1622 in various stages of restoration. John can tell you the archaeological back-story on any marine object in his lab.

On the workbench is a camera, a vacuum chamber for special handling, a microscope, and a tiny airscribe "jackhammer" for the skilled removal of artifact encrustations. There are also shelves of chemicals, storage tanks, a dehumidifier, and a 55-gallon drum of distilled water that John uses in his work. "Maintenance in the lab is never ending," John says.

When John received your piece-of-eight from the boat captain, he took a pre-conservation photo of it and updated the artifact database. As the corrosion began to lift from the coin, and identifying images could be seen, John reported that new data by virtue of the coin's identification number. Finally, when the conservation process was completed, he took a post-conservation photo of both sides of the coin and turned it over to Sandy Kavanaugh, the company's chief curator.

Sandy Kavanaugh came to the Fisher company in 2008 as a part-time employee in the inventory manager's office. In 2009 she was offered the position of curator and was trained on its database procedures. Her desk resembles a computer screen

Photo by Mel Fisher's Treasures

John Corcoran holds a restored gold plate from the Atocha *collection.*

fortress where she monitors and updates the records of almost every artifact that has ever been salvaged by the company. The numbered entries are in the hundreds of thousands.

When John Corcoran transfers an artifact from the conservation lab, Sandy photographs every coin and emerald, some for the second time, and enters all the detailed particulars into the database. Sandy herself assigns a grade status, based on set protocols, to each coin and then prints out a Certificate of Authenticity with its identification number, weight, grade, origin, and photos. The document is stamped and sealed with a security sticker that prevents the certificate from being replicated or machine copied. The coins and their documentation are then secured in a safe until they are released for division following adjudication by the Federal Court.

The handling of the *Atocha* emeralds follows a slightly different path. The logged gemstones are held to the end of the salvage season and then carefully weighed, graded, and appraised by one of the world's top experts in Muzo-mined emeralds, Manual Marcial. Once Sandy receives the reports on the emeralds, which includes their grades, weights, and current value, she enters the data into the computers, photographs each one, and Certificates of Authenticity are then prepared, completing the process of registering each emerald into the *Atocha* Collection.

The computer data program that Sandy manages was unique to archaeology when it was installed at an initial cost of $250,000. The updated program, which catalogues all the details of each numbered artifact, is essential to archaeologists for use in their interpretation of the historic shipwrecks. The Fisher-created program is still a world standard. Items pictured and described ranged from silver and gold coins, silver and copper ingots, silver jewel boxes, gold crosses and chains, rings set with emeralds, gold and coral rosaries, pendants and other jewelry, bronze and iron cannons, ship's iron hardware like locks and boat hooks, military weapons carried by soldiers, and navigational instruments carried by the pilots. Many other artifacts like pottery and tableware attest to the style and content of daily life. Each separate artifact presents a challenge to the conservators as well as to the archaeologists who must interpret them and provide a narrative story of their origins and use.

Investors in the Fisher company over the decades have not only underwritten the explorations for shipwreck treasures, but they have also helped to finance the company's archaeological

Sandy Kavanaugh, chief curator, oversees a world standard database for shipwreck artifacts.

preservation of artifacts and their historic documentation. Their rewards in the division of salvaged treasure are the original artifacts that they can proudly display in their homes or offices. Many wear their first Division piece-of-eight on a chain around their neck as a prized testament to their membership adventure.

There is someone else in the curator's department who has contributed a great deal to its operational legacy. Judy Sojourner Gracer, a bright, attractive, and energetic septuagenarian, is one of the company stalwarts still working today who was present for the discovery of the *Atocha* Mother Lode. Her path to joining the Fisher company began as a social interaction with Mel and Deo as members of a dinner party club. In 1982, Deo then asked Judy if she was available to help them at their floating *Golden Doubloon* treasure ship attraction that also served as their office space.

Her first job was taking tickets at the gangplank. Everyone liked Judy for her warm, generous personality and her infectious laugh, and she soon found herself named as Mel's executive secretary, doing expedition membership contract work and coordinating with the company's busy attorneys. Mel playfully gave Judy the title of "sex-a-tary."

Judy was literally in the middle of things when the *Atocha* Mother Lode was found in July 1985. The celebration and media excitement overflowed in the Greene Street office, and the crowd in Judy's administrative

Judy Sojourner Gracer, shown with Mel Fisher, as his administrative assistant in the 1980s, is still on the Fisher company staff.

office was so loud and pressing that Mel had to erect a cubicle with glass walls around Judy's desk so that she could work.

Judy remembers Mel as a funny, gregarious guy who could be very serious about his work. "When faced with a delay to something that he wanted done," Judy recalls, "Mel wouldn't wait. He'd do it himself."

Judy's favorite story about Mel involves her boss trying to carry a silver bar weighing about 80 pounds from his office to a small temporary conservation lab. Along his way, in view of the office staff, Mel's pants slipped off his waist and fell to his shoe tops. Balancing the heavy silver bar, Mel struggled out of one pants leg at a time to free himself, and then delivered the silver safely to the lab. He then put his pants back on with a burlesque-kind of dignity that has made Judy laugh whenever she remembers it.

In 1990, when Judy announced that she would marry Gene Gracer, a Miami businessman, Mel and Deo insisted on making their wedding part of the Fisher company Christmas party. The wedding invitations must have seemed odd. The invitation was not from parents, but from Treasure Salvors, Inc., and the location was not a church, but rather a Key West resort hotel. Judy remembers her wedding being observed by as many as 500 people who must have thought that she and Gene were movie stars.

The distance between Miami and Key West proved too difficult to manage by 1992, and Judy left the company. She admits that she missed Key West very much. Then in 1995, Deo asked Judy to return to the company as its curator, and she served in that department until 2007 when she retired at age 66. After the death of her husband, Judy was welcomed back into the family of Fisher company employees in 2011. Her schedule in this homecoming is three days a week with comfortable ten-to-five work hours.

Although her part-time job is in a support role in the curatorial department, no one better knows the operations of the company. When Judy programs curatorial information into the artifact database, she has probably performed this operation a thousand times before. And when she works directly with the long-term expedition members, they can laugh together at the many fun times they have shared over the years.

At special events that celebrate the Fisher company, Judy proudly wears an *Atocha* Mother Lode Golden Crew Ring numbered 14.

Every year the division committee will oversee that each artifact is assigned a number of points based on its value. This information is entered into the computer, and the computer selects specific artifacts to match the points due each member. Following the annual adjudication of title, the treasure is released to the members in a spectacular gala that lasts a full week. The remaining treasure will find its way to the already heavily laden coffers of the Mel Fisher company. From here some of the treasures will be delivered to Star Fisher, the retail store inventory manager.

Star came into the Fisher family by marriage to Kim's son Sean in 2000. Ten years ago, in a move to Key West, Star joined the company. Star will prepare

Star Fisher, with her dog Bucci nearby, manages the treasure inventory for retail sale.

234

some of the treasure to be received by the two retail stores in Key West, one at the 200 Greene Street location and the other at Mel Fisher's Treasures, 613 1/2 Duval St. Some treasure will be available through the Mel Fisher online store, and some will be sent to the Mel Fisher Museum located in Sebastian, Florida. The Sebastian location was managed by Kim Fisher's sister, Taffi Fisher Abt, for 25 years, and now her daughter Nichole Abt is carrying on the family tradition.

Since the Fisher company has been making divisions of pieces-of-eight since the early 1960s, which includes the thousands of coins from the *Atocha* Mother Lode in the 1980s, the numismatic records of their activity had spanned over 50 years by 2015. Who else has documented more on the coinage of Spanish colonialism in the Americas? Who would you trust more to provide you with such unique masterpieces of our collective intercontinental history?

42

The *Atocha* Coin Market

THE WORD ATOCHA HAS become a brand name for manufacturers to cash in on the accomplishments of the greatest shipwreck recovery in world history. The story of the *Atocha* discovery has passed into legendary status due to the many newspaper and magazine feature articles, the National Geographic television documentaries, and a half-dozen books that propelled it into public consciousness. Link the name "Mel Fisher" with the word *Atocha*, and most adults of perhaps three generations will recall enough details about the shipwreck and treasure to earn points in a trivia contest.

Serious collectors in the numismatic marketplace know the vast difference between a certified authentic piece-of-eight from the *Atocha* and a replica. Some replica coins made with silver from the *Atocha* come with a Certificate of Authenticity that provides the silver ingot bar number and the *Atocha* manifest number. A one-reale replica coin pendant of this type of modern manufacture in 2014 ranged in price from $70 to $175.

By contrast, a four-reales pre-Mother Lode *Atocha* coin adjudicated for division by the State of Florida in 1975, with a Certificate of Authenticity signed personally by Mel Fisher, Deo Fisher, Eugene Lyon and Duncan Mathewson, was offered in 2014 for $9,500. The certificate, with its celebrity treasure salvor autographs, has value itself as a historic document. As time passes, there may also be a distinction on how your *Atocha* coin was acquired.

If you were a boat captain, diver, archaeologist, conservator, curator, Fisher company employee, or an expedition member who received your piece-of-eight in an annual division of treasure, your ownership attests to your personal role in the historic adventure. If it is then transferred by your estate to family members, or offered for public sale, the specific coin nevertheless has a direct connection to the original salvors. That fact may provide added value to the artifact. The excitement about owning an authentic piece of the *Atocha* treasure is in the story that you can tell about it.

At some point in the future, as any marine archaeologist will tell you, all of the 1622 Spanish galleon fleet shipwreck treasures that can be found and recovered will reside in museums or in the private collections of individuals. These artifacts are finite in number, and one day there will be no more of them available for sale. What will it feel like then to hold these *Atocha* relics in one's hands?

43

The Mel Fisher Maritime Museum

THE ICONIC BUILDING AT the heart of Key West's Old Town Historic District began as a U.S. Navy warehouse in 1911 in support of the Key West Navy base and its Truman Annex. The five-story construction of steel and concrete was built to last, and it served the Navy until the base closed in 1975. It was acquired by the Fisher company in 1984 to serve as its corporate headquarters, conservation laboratory, and museum.

The genesis of the Mel Fisher Maritime Museum was begun in 1982 with the founding of The Mel Fisher Maritime Heritage Society, a 501(c) (3) accredited not-for-profit organization "existing for the purpose of accumulating and disseminating information; providing education services to the public on maritime and colonial activity in the New World, and preserving maritime cultural resources."

Mel Fisher and his wife Deo recognized the need to establish a means to preserve the legacy of their historic discoveries. The society, and the museum that it founded, thus became the

vehicle for that shared vision. The intention was to retain a permanent home for the Atocha Collection in Key West that could
be enjoyed by future generations. In 1986 the Board of Treasure Salvors, Inc. dissolved the company and Mel transferred
(donated) much of his share of the recoveries to the non-profit
heritage museum. Among the artifacts were the most prized:
the largest emerald recovered, a gold poison cup, and a stunning
gold-and-emerald cross. The visionary insightfulness that Mel
and Deo Fisher exhibited has been rewarded for over 25 years as
more than 200,000 people a year visit the museum.

Although the primary focus of the museum is on the 1622
Spanish galleon treasure fleet and on the rich recoveries from
the *Atocha* and *Santa Margarita*, the museum operates a separate
2,000-square foot conservation laboratory and continues to
make additions to its collection of more than 100,000 artifacts.

One of the surprises for visitors in the museum is the extensive
exhibition coverage of The *Henrietta Marie*, an English merchant
slave ship that sank 35 miles west of Key West in the summer of
1700. The ship had just sold its 190 captive Africans into slavery
in Jamaica. While searching for the *Atocha*, Fisher company salvors
found the *Henrietta Marie* in 1972, but it was not worked by company archaeologists until 1983. Although it was not a treasure ship,
it was recognized as an important piece of our maritime heritage.

All of the artifacts recovered by a Fisher-sponsored salvage
operation were donated to the Heritage Society. They included
iron shackles and a cast bronze bell etched with the name "The
Henrietta Marie" and the date "1699." The discovery became the
earliest slave ship ever identified by name. This identification
allowed researchers to use historic records to reconstruct a little
known period in American history. In 1995, the Mel Fisher Maritime Museum produced "A Slave Ship Speaks," the first major

museum exhibition in the USA devoted to the transatlantic slave trade. The exhibition then toured to museums across the USA under the sponsorship of the General Motors Corporation.

The executive leadership of the Mel Fisher Maritime Museum has impressive credentials and long records of service to its goals and operations. Melissa Kendrick, the Executive Director, began her association with the museum in 1991 as Director of Finance and Development. Her educational background includes a degree in Finance from New York University.

The day-to-day administration of the museum involves a staff of about 15 employees. The extension of the museum's education and preservation activities now also includes the Key West Turtle Museum.

Another long-term leader of the museum is Corey Malcom, the Director of Archaeology. Corey earned his initial degree in Anthropology/Archaeology at Indiana University. After completing a master's degree in 2009, he has pursued his Ph.D at the University of Huddersfield in England. As an assistant archaeologist in 1986, working under the supervision of Duncan Mathewson, Corey worked on excavation and data recovery at the *Atocha* and *Santa Margarita* shipwreck sites. In 1988 he was the project archaeologist for survey and excavation work at the shipwreck site of the *Nuestra Señora de la Concepcion*, a Spanish Manila galleon wrecked in 1638. In 1991 he was the project archaeologist for the survey and excavation of the now exhibited English merchant-slaver the *Henrietta Marie*. Into the new century Corey has served as the principal investigator on additional shipwreck projects. His skills now include remote sensing surveys of reefs and other underwater sites, and ground-penetrating radar surveys of beaches. The archaeological expertise of the maritime museum and its conservation laboratory seems to always be in demand.

Another example of professional growth at the museum is Monica Brook, the Chief Conservator. Monica joined the museum staff as a conservation intern in 1997. She was then a recent graduate of the Collections, Conservation, and Management Program at Sir Sandford Fleming College in Ontario, Canada. Monica then advanced by experience to the title of Conservation Technician, and finally to her role in 2000 as the department head with responsibility for the conservation of recovered artifacts and the preservation and care of the museum's collections.

These three leaders, their staff members, and the many museum patrons are maintaining and growing the museum's preservation and educational mission.

The best-informed visitors who wander through the *Atocha* exhibits can still imagine encountering the great visionary explorer himself as so many people did in these very spaces. Yet, although Mel Fisher has passed, there are still living people who can tell the *Atocha* story of exploration and discovery from first-hand experience. Perhaps during a museum visit, you might encounter Kim Fisher, or Andy Matroci or Jim Sinclair, or someone else who wears the Golden Crew ring. History lives on the lips of these witnesses to a great adventure that still fires our imagination today.

To see all the maritime wonders found by the Fisher company, you can visit the Key West museum daily. It should be noted that the museum does not sell authentic coins from the 1622 Fleet shipwreck. It displays authentic coins in exhibits, but it sells only museum-quality replica coins in its gift shop. The real coins with their Certificate of Authenticity are available for sale in the Fisher company retail store, which has a side entrance on Front Street across from the Hyatt Hotel parking garage and the cruise ships pier.

44

Adjudication Day

THE DAY OF ADJUDICATION of title in the United States District Court for the Southern District of Florida is a red-letter day at Mel Fisher's Treasures. All the participants who normally work in shorts, shirts, and sandals come to work that day with a suit bag and dress shoes. Proper attire is required to enter the courtroom. All the treasures salvaged the previous year have been preserved and stored by Mel Fisher's Treasures as substitute custodians of the court. Today, in open court, the treasure inventory logbooks and the treasure itself will be shown to the judge who will adjudicate title to the recoveries from the previous year.

Senior Judge James Lawrence King is the longest serving Federal judge in the history of the United States. In 1970, Republican President Richard Nixon was preparing his nominations for the Federal bench and was expected to list a full slate of Republicans. The U.S. Senate that was controlled by the Democrats, however, warned Nixon that it would not approve any Republican nominees unless they were preceded by nominations of Democrat judges. The favorite judge being promoted by a powerful coalition of Southern Democratic senators was a brilliant young 43-year-old judge named James Lawrence King. That year, Judge King was the first Federal judge confirmed by the Senate.

Judge King's distinguished career was honored by the Federal judiciary when the U.S. Courthouse in Miami was named the James Lawrence King Federal Justice Building.

With regard to decisions pertaining to the Fisher family, in 1981 Judge King overruled the State of Florida in determining that treasure hunter Mel Fisher was the rightful owner of treasure salvaged from the 1715 Spanish galleon fleet. Judge King ruled that Federal admiralty law superseded state law.

Kim, Lee, attorney Gene Lewis, and Gary Randolph on the courthouse steps after another successful adjudication.

For the last 35 years, Judge King has presided over the Fisher treasure adjudication hearing that is held in the Key West Federal Courthouse. In late April of 2014, the immaculately groomed white-haired judge entered the courtroom. He appeared relaxed and poised at 87 years old after the 168-mile trip from Miami. Judge King appears to like coming to Key West for the adjudication hearing after a steady court docket of violent crimes and illegal drug cases. Judge King had a history of presiding over many landmark cases, some that necessitated U. S. Marshal protection for his personal security.

Judge King told Kim that he respected the manner in which the Fisher family had archived and conserved their salvaged treasure. He also appreciated the public access to the unique artifacts and the historical perspective provided at the Mel Fisher Maritime Heritage Museum.

After Gene Lewis, the Fisher corporate attorney, officially presented the treasure inventory documents and made his motions, Kim was sworn in to give his testimony. Kim addressed the judge and recapped the chain of search, salvage, and conservation of the treasure artifacts recovered during 2013. After Kim's testimony, Judge King signed the order of title and then came down from the bench to inspect a table display of artifacts recovered from the *Atocha*. Kim was at his side to describe the items and to respond to any questions. Clearly, the judge was enjoying his close-up inspection of the gold, silver, and emerald items valued in the millions of dollars.

Then the judge did an unusual thing. He invited Lee and the rest of the folks in the gallery to come into the inner court to view the treasure and to meet him. Judge King greeted each individual with a handshake and paused to give each one a personal moment of conversation. His natural charm was both obvious and genuine. The entire event from "all rise" to the withdrawal of the judge to his chambers lasted only 25 minutes.

Kim and Lee had been greeted warmly by the judge, and their goodbye wish was for his good health and the opportunity of seeing him again next year. Next year when he would be 88.

Shawn Cowles, Investor Relations Manager,
joined Mel Fisher's Treasures in 1992.

45

Keys to the Treasure

AMONG THE 33 INDIVIDUALS listed on the executive and staff roster of Mel Fisher's Treasures, there are key people who have a long history with the company. One of these in 2014 was Shawn Cowles, the Investor Relations Manager. Shawn, a Western Massachusetts native, took up scuba diving at an early age and became certified at age 12. In junior college, he wrote a paper on the treasure-hunting exploits of Mel Fisher and his finding of the *Atocha* Mother Lode. In 1992, on his spring break from college, Shawn made his way to Key West with the express purpose of meeting his hero. He tracked Mel down at the Schooner Wharf Bar and asked for an opportunity to join his salvage operation.

Shawn then returned to Massachusetts, but not to continue college. He sold whatever would not travel, and with barely $200, he came back to Key West. His first accommodation was a sofa bed that he rented by the month. Soon, however, he secured a job as a diver on a search boat that Mel had contracted. Shawn continued his education during those early years by completing an associate degree in Diving Business and Technology, a unique science course offered at Florida Keys Community College.

By 1994, Shawn was diving for emeralds, and he found hundreds of them. At age 22, without family obligations, he was living a young man's adventure dream. One week Mel gave Shawn a $50 bonus check for exceeding his quota of emeralds, but in the excitement of divers on shore leave, he lost the check. Fifty dollars twenty years ago probably had the buying power of $150 today. It was no slight loss, but Shawn was too embarrassed to ask Mel for a remake.

Years passed, and Shawn worked as a diver in deepwater mixed gas treasure searches all over the world. He also made promotional tours with Mel, where they would set up displays of the *Atocha* story with its valuable artifacts and then offer authenticated gold and silver coins from the shipwreck in a retail environment. Shawn personally designed for Kim and Lee an exhibit of *Atocha* treasures on affluent Sanibel Island and manned its retail operations there for three years.

After Mel Fisher died at the end of 1998, Shawn found the $50 check that Mel had given him nearly five years before. He could not bring himself to cash it. He considered it an heirloom.

Shawn Cowles was the natural choice to lead the development of Investor Relations at Mel Fisher's Treasures with his experience about the adventures associated with the *Atocha* and the *Santa Margarita*. In his twelve years as the head of Investor Relations, Shawn has turned the annual division of treasure artifacts into Division Week Extravaganza. Since 2002, expedition members and their families have come to Key West to not only claim their share of the treasure found the previous year, but also to participate in a gala week of dive opportunities, tours, and nightly parties.

Old friends who have been members for ten years or more are united for a week of celebration. For them, Division Week is also one of the reasons that they will renew their memberships for the coming year. They want to continue their membership in this very exciting club.

The Mel Fisher's Expedition membership, whether you are a diver or not, includes year-round privileges to participate in the treasure hunt at sea on the salvage boats. Members who are certified divers are permitted to dive with the crew and search for treasure.

For non-divers, there are three weeks of special opportunities for them to visit Emerald City, a prime *Atocha* site where hundreds of emeralds have been previously found. During Division Week in May, Mel Fisher Days in July, and a September week, members can sift through sediment flooding into sluice boxes. Divers below are sending up the sand mixed with shells and emeralds via an airlift. The airlift brings the potential emerald treasure to trays on deck where they can be sifted through and discovered by the members. The emerald mines at Muzo, Colombia produce the world standard for emerald color, size, and clarity. They are the highest quality emeralds in the world. In the years 1620 through 1622, there occurred the largest recovery of emeralds in the mine's history. Thus it is likely that the quantity of emeralds shipped on the *Atocha* was greater than any other year. The temptation to buy gemstones and smuggle them from this historic bounty of emeralds must have been overwhelming to the royals and wealthy merchants who were returning to Spain. Perhaps that is why the Emerald City dive site continues to surprise and amaze, as it produces emeralds year after year.

Kim had a very memorable dive in 1986 while searching in 55 feet of water near the main *Atocha* site. It was a beautiful calm sea day, and the water was crystal clear. When Kim's metal detector alerted him to an object in the mud, he hand fanned it to expose what came to be identified as a silver salt dish. Kim them employed a 20-ft. long airlift pipe to carefully explore the area around the salt dish. All of a sudden, the pipe began to rattle as a quantity of emeralds shot up the airlift. Seeing emeralds, Kim turned off the suction, but already the water above him was filled with them. They came down in a shower, and Kim grasped for them as they floated by. There were emeralds even in his hair.

For the remainder of his dive time, Kim picked up emeralds off the ocean bottom. The gems were the very valuable dark green Muzo emeralds from three to ten karats each. Kim's recovery of *Atocha* emeralds that day were later valued at over $1 million.

There is nothing equally exciting as to be at sea on the stern working deck of a 90-foot Fisher salvage boat when the flood of sediment passing through the sluice boxes brings up a startling green emerald. The finder yells with delight, the others cheer, and the boat's bell is rung loud enough so that even the diver working the airlift below can hear it and intensify his search. Back in Key West at a Division Week party, there will be many fellow investors who eagerly want to hear the most recent stories of discovery.

In 2014 Sharon Drager, Marketing Manager; Jan Stauch, Finance Manager; Star Fisher, Inventory Manager; and Shawn Cowles joined forces to become the primary special-event planners for Division Week. They were supported, of course, by every staff member on the Fisher company team. The scope of Division Week events would challenge any professional in the event staging field. Over their combined years in Key West, the event production team has developed a large network of skilled and talented local professionals to help them stage memorable events. The roster of dependable resources must include "the best of the best" as Sharon tells it. They must be the best caterers, the best entertainers, the best costume makers, the best courtyard decorators, and the best musicians in the Keys. The calling for all these performers and providers is to create a wonderful week of fun, romance and adventure as a way to celebrate, entertain, and thank the expedition members. Anything less is unacceptable.

Division Week also involves every member of the organizational team. Every individual from Joe Sweeney, Administrative Director, to boat captains Papo José Garcia and Andy Matroci will play roles in hosting the members and their families. Kim and Lee, as the primary hosts, must be gracious greeters throughout the day to late-night itinerary beginning with a Monday Mel Fisher Museum Courtyard party and ending with a Sunday Decompression Brunch.

The theme of the 2014 Division Week was Into The Blue: Secrets of the Deep. The highlight was a costumed gala for a guest list of 400 on the beach of the Casa Marina Resort. In addition to theatrical and musical entertainments, the winner of the costume contest received a Grade One *Atocha* coin valued at $2,800. The grand party included appetizers, dinner, and drinks. It was typical of how the Fisher organization stages first-class events both on land and at the *Atocha* dive site at sea.

46

Division Week

BEFORE DIVISION WEEK CAN be celebrated by the Fisher company and its investor members, a great deal of preparation is required. The mid-May annual dates mark the ending of one treasure search season and the beginning of another. Down at the docks Captain Andy Matroci of the *JB Magruder* and Captain José "Papo" Garcia of the M/V *Dare* are preparing their vessels for expedition member dive trips to the *Atocha* site and for non-divers to search for emeralds vacuumed up into sluice boxes from the always-productive Emerald City site. Kim and attorney Gene Lewis are preparing to go into Judge King's Federal District Court for adjudication day and the release of the previous year's salvaged treasure. Meanwhile, Chief Curator Sandy Kavanaugh, with support from Investor Relations and other company departments, is working her database to complete the details of the division of the treasure to members.

In the executive office, administrator Joe Sweeney is busy booking individual Division appointments where members will actually receive their shares of the recovered treasures. He also schedules their dive trips and Emerald City trips during their stay in Key West. Scuba divers who want to go to sea must be certified and also qualified by the company to be fit enough for the physicality of the adventure. For example, transferring from the taxi boat to the salvage vessel can be challenging, so Joe tactfully asks about the individual guest's ability to climb a ladder on a rocking boat. Of course, any trip forty miles out into the ocean to the treasure grounds is always dependent on weather and sea conditions. Safety is the primary concern, so boat captains and the executive office constantly monitor tides, currents, visibility, and sea conditions before any guest member leaves the dock.

In May, the storms of winter have passed, and the Atlantic Ocean off the Florida coast calms except for the occasional fronts that sweep across the Gulf of Mexico from the west. The window of opportunity for treasure hunters during the next few months calls for an all-out effort of seamen and their boats. They must work each precious clear and warm-water day from dawn to sunset. They must find treasure before the hurricanes come. In Kim Fisher's Division Week report to his expedition members, he summarizes the task ahead.

"Both the *Magruder* and the *Dare* have been able to go out to sea between cold fronts this spring and are in optimal condition to ensure a productive 2014 summer.

We have completed our modifications and upgrades to *Dolores* and will continue to work for a number of weeks on the *Atocha* site immediately following Division Week. We will survey the main pile of the *Atocha* with *Dolores* in search of the remaining heavy cargo such as cannons, chest of coins, and silver bars. After acquiring numerous targets on the *Atocha* site, we will send the

Dare along with *Dolores* back to northern Florida to accomplish our goal of finding the Lost Merchant shipwreck.

We will be using *Dolores* in AUV mode as well as using our towed system for survey. This will allow us to cover more area in less time. We appreciate your patience, perseverance and commitment and invite all of you to participate in the 2014 Expedition. With the reduced survey "box" on the Lost Merchant project and the modifications and upgrades made to *Dolores*, we believe that 2014 will be a rewarding year."

Most of the members in the group already knew what their leader Kim had reported. They already knew because they followed the company's activity on its website and through communications with Fisher staff members whom they knew on a first-name basis. They knew because they came to Key West more than once a year to dive, fish, party, and get personally updated on treasure salvage expectations. In this way, they felt that they were participants in one of the greatest exploration adventures of their lifetime. Now, during Division Week, the focus of their participation could be celebrated with their fellow expedition members and with the daring men and women who were actualizing their dreams. What good is any degree of wealth, they would collectively agree, if it cannot generate some adventurous fun? Division Week in Key West definitely came through on the fun factor year after year. The treasure that members claimed in their Division appointments came as a bonus. It was fun and excitement manifested into something that you could hold and display.

Expedition members enjoy their personal relationship with the company by following a constant flow of its activities at *www.melfisher.com*. The website provides text, video, and blogs that keep members both advised and connected. The flow of information is managed by Sharon Drager, the company's public relations specialist. When newspaper, magazine, television, and cable media want to do stories on the Fisher company, Sharon makes the arrangements and serves as their on-deck guide. She has thus appeared in dozens of filmed interviews. When members are on board and willing, they, too, become part of the news story being filmed that day. The camera is always eager to document the excitement of another emerald find or the recovery of another piece-of-eight. And if there is no National Geographic Society camera on hand to capture your treasure find of a lifetime, there is always the cellphone camera "selfie."

47

The Consolation Prize

THE SPECIAL EVENTS OF Division Week open on Monday with a 6 to 8 p.m. reception in the large Mel Fisher Maritime Museum Courtyard. Kim and Lee, as hosts, greet their expedition member guests, and the camaraderie is evident as old friendships are renewed and new ones begun. The members of the "club" who underwrote the 2013 treasure search have a unique relationship with the Fisher family, its boat captains, divers, Investor Relations staff, and headquarters team. Some of them have come to receive their share of the year's discoveries for more than 15 years and have watched each other's children grow up in the process.

The courtyard party weather was perfect, warm with a slight breeze. The long buffet table under the banyan trees was loaded with more than reception fare. Two trips through, and there was no need to eat out afterwards. Sharon Drager, who carries the title of marketing manager, is the principal hands-on event planner for the Division Week events. She, with the key assistance of everyone in the finance, inventory, curating, investor relations, retail sales, and security departments, took care of every hospitality detail. They worked diligently every afternoon for weeks preceding the courtyard party on the Key West punch that would be served at the open bar. It was their special recipe. It was blue like the Division Week theme: Into The Blue. It was tropical, slightly sweet, and suddenly intoxicating. Just what the guests and crew expected.

Sharon and team had designed a contest to facilitate the interaction of the members with each other as they gathered that evening. A small 4 1/4 x 5 1/2-inch card had a list of questions that were to be answered by other members. The first member to complete the contest list would win a valuable *Atocha* coin. There were only five questions on each card, but not all cards had the same questions. Here is a sample of the winning card.

Kim presents New Yorker Vic Cipullo with his consolation prize.

MEL FISHER'S EXPEDITIONS

Your name: _____

1. Find someone who met Mel Fisher_____

2. Find someone who is an only child _____

3. Find someone who is good at math _____

4. Find someone who knows the date (M/D/Y) Mel found the Motherlode_____

5. Find someone who drank coffee at breakfast today_____

Here is perhaps a more difficult card to complete:

MEL FISHER'S EXPEDITIONS

Your name:_____

1. Find someone who has been diving on the Atocha site_____

2. Find someone who can name 3 members of the Fisher family

_____

3. Find someone who is good at math_____

4. Find someone who has completed a 5K_____

5. Find someone who knows how to ballroom dance_____

With Investor Relations Manager Shawn Cowles serving as emcee on the front steps of the Museum, he announced a contest winner. The crowd gathered around the steps, and Vic Cipullo, a retired, highly decorated New York City police detective, stood beside Shawn as the individuals on Vic's list identified themselves. Then came a hitch. The question asking the exact date of the finding of the *Atocha* Mother Lode did not list the person who provided the answer, but rather the answer itself—July 20, 1985. Vic, unfortunately, was disqualified, and the next person with a completed list won the prize.

The next morning Kim and Lee discussed Vic Cipullo's courtyard disappointment. Kim went to the safe that contained their personal collection, selected a coin with its certificate of authenticity, and had Joe Sweeney prepare it in a presentation folder. That afternoon Kim sought out Vic who had his Division appointment in the Investor Relations office. Vic was completely surprised when Kim awarded him a "consolation" contest prize. It was a coin of equal value to the one given to the winner on the previous night.

Sharon was on hand with her camera to document the event, and she would send the photo as an attachment to Vic's e-mail address so that he would have that, too, as a keepsake. It was a courtesy and kindness that she would extend to all the members. She would take posed and candid professional photos of them and made sure that they received copies.

The consolation prize anecdote goes to demonstrate how much the Fisher organization values its expedition members. For the members, too, it's more than the money. It's about friendship and participation in an ongoing historic adventure that is recognized around the world.

48

Feeling Part of It

ON VALENTINE'S WEEKEND, FEBRUARY 2010, Phil "Boot" Le Boutillier was attending the Miami Boat Show when he noticed the Mel Fisher's Treasures booth. Phil, whose heritage is seafaring, has homes in West Palm Beach and Elbow Cay, Abaco Island in the Bahamas. He's a sports fisherman, seaside resort owner, and a Bahamian wooden boat restorer, so he had a natural interest in seafaring subjects like shipwreck treasure.

Phil is a man of few words and is built like an NFL linebacker. He is not to be trifled with in frivolous conversation. When encountering him, one should quickly get to the point and avoid extravagance. Who would figure that Phil Le Boutillier has the soul of an adventurer?

The Investor Relations staff members manning the booth in Miami could not have guessed that the imposing man standing in front of their exhibit would become a major sponsor of future expeditions. Phil admits that the *Atocha* Mother Lode story and the displayed treasure artifacts fascinated him. When he heard

*Phil "Boot" Le Boutillier and his wife Kent pose
with Lee and Kim during Division Week.*

the details of becoming an expedition member in the coming summer's search for the *Atocha* sterncastle, he says that he realized immediately that participation in treasure hunting was not like investing in the stock market. If he wanted to join the expedition, he understood, he would have to be in it for the excitement, not for the profit.

"I was never in it for the money," Phil says. "I recognized the Fisher organization as both first class and high tech. I wanted to meet these people and join their adventure. That was my entire motivation."

Despite some lean treasure years since joining in 2010, Phil says, "I'm overwhelmed by the treasures that I have received. And as long as I don't sell my *Atocha* artifacts, I pay no taxes to own and enjoy them."

During Division Week in 2014, Phil was accompanied by his wife Kent, a charming woman who hosts their small resort, named Tomato Paste, in the Bahamas. Their primary home in

West Palm Beach is only a direct commercial flight of 175 miles east to the airport on Great Abaco, where they catch a ferry ride to Hope Town Harbor and then take a five-minute private boat ride to Tomato Paste. Individuals who choose this lifestyle might rightfully be called "island people."

Kent had accompanied Phil on this trip to Key West to accept a gift from her husband. As a significant member, Phil had accumulated enough points to entitle him to a major artifact. His choice was a single emerald that would be designed and crafted by Manuel Marcial of Key West Emeralds International into a dazzling piece of jewelry.

Looking toward the next expedition season, Phil says, "I have total confidence in our discovery future. The *Dolores* technology is something fantastic, and I feel part of it. I'm a participating partner in the making of history. Not many people can say that. This is the way that I have fun these days."

*Expedition member Gary Simon
with a palm full of emeralds.*

49

The Cigar Box

GARY SIMON GREW UP on the Chesapeake Bay in Norfolk, Virginia and went to Old Dominion University where he was introduced to marine archaeology and became scuba certified. He later graduated from the University of North Carolina. As a coin collector who especially valued the historic background of his artifacts, Gary gravitated to the numismatics of the Civil War and other earlier epochs in American history.

When his family vacation cruise ship docked for excursions in Key West in 2012, Gary saw The Mel Fisher Maritime Museum as a stimulating place of interest. He had already read widely about coinage associated with the Spanish colonial empire in the Americas; and as a professional jeweler, he was also excited to see the emeralds from the legendary Muzo mines in Colombia that were recovered from the *Atocha*. One of them on display was a huge 77 carats.

His interest in uncirculated *Atocha* coins led him to a conversation with Shawn Cowles in the Investor Relations office adjacent

.o the Fisher company retail jewelry store. Shawn invited Gary to lift a solid silver bar and to wear a heavy gold chain recovered from the *Atocha*. Gary admits to being thrilled by the handling of such historic artifacts. Then Shawn arranged for a private tour of the conservation lab with conservator John Corcoran. The experience of entering the lab was like stepping through a portal of time as he found himself surrounded by shelves and water-filled tanks loaded with shipwreck artifacts being prepared for their debut after 400 years resting on the ocean floor. That encounter propelled Gary into becoming an expedition member. He wanted more. Gary wanted to be part of the team experiencing the discoveries and adventures for himself.

"Becoming part of the Fisher search and conservation community offered me a basketful of things that interested me most," Gary says.

In 2013 Gary found himself cruising through the clear shallow Caribbean blue-green waters alongside Captain Andy Matroci aboard the salvage vessel *JB Magruder* enroute to the *Atocha's* famous "Emerald City" site. Millions of dollars in Muzo emeralds were still waiting to be airlifted onto the deck's unique sluice boxes where crew and members could pick them out from the rushing sediment. "Today was the Day" for Gary to find his first of his four Muzo emeralds.

"It is a very special feeling to find an emerald with your own eyes on the *Atocha* site. As a jeweler, I recognized the quality of a Muzo gemstone. Today that first-found emerald is mounted on the *Atocha* coin that I wear around my neck. My first Division coin was an eight-Reale, Grade 2 coin minted in Potosi, Peru prior to 1622. The face of the coin depicts with strong relief the shield of the Spanish crown half visible and half sea worn from almost 400 years of submerged shifting sands and currents. Each coin is registered into the *Atocha* collection and comes with a Certificate of Authenticity proving an unbroken chain of provenance."

Gary collects Mel Fisher coins and artifacts from the *Atocha* and the *Santa Margarita* as well as the 1715 Fleet that he displays in the customer consulting office of his Simon Jewelers store in High Point, North Carolina. There is a much more modern artifact, however, that gets a lot of attention, especially from fellow Fisher company expedition members. It is a wooden cigar box, 11 by 7 by 5 inches deep circa 1985. The box lid has the brand name ink-screened on its left side. The bold lettering reads, "Treasure Hunter Cigars." The central panel shows a photo-like ink screen of Mel Fisher dressed in his robe and crown as the King of the Conch Republic. He is sitting on a throne with a long cigar in his hand behind a table filled with gold bars and gold chains. He appears very joyful. On the right side of the lid, Mel's motto "Today's the Day" appears over a facsimile of his signature.

The cigar box is well made with dovetailed corners, and inked into its front panel is more celebration of the treasure ship's Mother Lode. The design features an old-style lettering announcing "Nuestra Senora de Atocha" and three bold pieces-of-eight coin fronts. Below, out of a curtained stage-like setting, the *Atocha* itself sails bow first in all her glory. The date 1622 prominently appears, and the bottom of the design is anchored by the horizontal rendering of a salvaged gold bar.

Gary found the dust-covered cigar box in a Key West curio shop. He does not know how many of these boxes were produced or the quality of the cigars that they contained. He treasures it, however, because it is a relic of a time in Key West when Mel Fisher made shipwreck treasure history by discovering the legendary 1622 *Nuestra Señora de Atocha*, and celebration cigars were smoked throughout the Keys.

50

A Pocket Emerald

ON THE FOURTH DAY of Division Week, Kim and Lee spent the morning with a major long-term expedition member and his wife. One of their objectives was to select an emerald or two for the division. Before noon, they adjourned to the private office of one of the world's greatest experts and designer of emerald jewelry, Manuel Marcial, to have the emeralds evaluated and appraised. The members then made their selection, and the two couples went to lunch together.

Kim, as always, was wearing shorts and sandals; and before hosting a private dinner event for Emerald-Level expedition members, he made an appearance at the Smokin Tuna Saloon, where other members and staff were having a treasure Booty Bingo Party complete with live music, food and drinks, and a belly-laughs bingo game.

Still in shorts and looking the epitome of Key West comfortable and relaxed, Kim with Lee, who wore a long tropical dress, ate dinner and interacted with their most supportive members. When they returned home after ten that night, Kim removed items from his pants pockets, the way men often do at the end of a long day, and he discovered that he had been carrying the one emerald that the member couple had not selected. It had been in his pants pocket all day from before noon. Its value was over $600,000.00.

The next morning, back at his office, the large gemstone was returned to a company safe. Again, it was produced from Kim's pants pocket as casually as if it had been a quarter. There was, of course, no danger of loss, but who other than a successful treasure hunter could be so relaxed walking around with a fortune in his pocket?

Kim also wears a large *Atocha* coin medallion around his neck every day. Its size and position at the center of his chest often attracts second looks. Some people even mistake Kim for a gold-shield police detective with his badge-size jewelry. What would they think if they knew that Kim had a large emerald in his pocket?

51

The Golden Girl

In 1996 Jean Thornton had no idea that her life would radically change when she was introduced to Mel Fisher during a visit to his Key West museum. Jean was a middle-aged English teacher who was introducing computer technology to the Birmingham, Alabama school system. She had met her husband Joe in 1967 while on a study program in Scotland and had then joined him at the University of Alabama, where they graduated, married, and became lifelong "Roll Tide" football fans. Her life in 1996 was comfortable and conventional. Joe was successful as a manufacturer's representative for electric power equipment, and they had two children who were doing well. Key West, for them, was maybe a vacation destination, certainly not yet a lifestyle.

Jean was vacationing with a girlfriend when she encountered Mel. She and Mel connected that they were both born in Indiana, and that Jean's mother had Fisher as her maiden name. Mel treated both women to a personal tour of the museum, and then they were photographed in gold chains from the *Atocha*. Before they left, the women had used their credit cards to finance an expedition membership, and Jean had assured Mel that she would take lessons and become scuba qualified so that she could dive on the *Atocha* the following summer.

True to her word, Jean made her first dive on the *Atocha* in July. The gold coin that she now wears everyday was found on that dive as well as a long gold chain. Her exceptional luck caused Mel and the boat crew to christen Jean "the Golden Girl."

"Finding that gold got me hooked on diving," Jean says. "It also changed me as a person. Mel and I became friends, and he inspired me to follow my dreams. I was told by my new friends never to tell Mel that something cannot be done. If you did, he would take you into his office and force you to work with him on a solution. There will never be another person like Mel."

When Jean met Mel, he was already in the late stages of his bladder cancer. Then, in December 1998, Mel died. Although Jean had known Mel for only two years, she attended his memorial service in Key West and then made a momentous decision. After a career of 28 years in teaching, Jean retired to follow her dreams, and with Joe's support, she spent two six-week periods a year with the Fisher organization where she worked at whatever needed to be done. The proceeds from this employment were reinvested to maintain Jean's status as a member. Eventually, the Thorntons would purchase a condominium in the Truman Annex, a short walk to the Fishers' Greene Street headquarters, as a base for Jean's involvement.

Jean's personality and poise made her a natural choice to front for the company when filmmakers wanted to showcase the Mel Fisher Expedition experience. Pat Clyne, then the company vice president, asked Jean to participate in the BBC filming of a program devoted to "women living dangerously." In Jean's underwater scenes, she was operating the airlift to suck up bottom sediment that might contain coins or emeralds. Jean had always had a problem with equalizing her ear pressure during a dive. Especially in strong underwater currents, she would experience vertigo and start to vomit. As recorded by the BBC, Jean got vertigo, began vomiting, and fought heroically to regain the surface. "What a show!" the camera crew agreed. That trip in 2001 also miraculously produced the recovery of many gold bars and silver coins.

In another filming for the Travel Channel in April 2002, Jean was asked to be one of three members to do a pretend "division" as part of the program storytelling. Jean's treasure for the benefit of the filming was a big *Atocha* emerald. Back at the office, Jean kidded Kim that she deserved a big emerald. Then, within a week, Jean was working on the salvage vessel *Dauntless* in support of an Emerald City trip for a boatload of expedition members who were sifting for emeralds in the sluice boxes. Jean decided to try her luck underwater, and so she went over the side to swim a circular search pattern. Within

Jean Thornton shows off her find of a large emerald.

her field of vision Jean saw a beautiful shell that would make a nice gift, so she swam to recover it. Next to the shell she saw something that froze her in place and took her breath away. It was a huge emerald, a deep green gemstone of 27.74 carats. Excited beyond words, Jean surfaced with the emerald, but she could not get the crew's attention. To regain the deck by ladder, she put the large gem into the top of her dive glove where it appeared as an unsightly hump. Finally, she reached the deck and got the attention of the members and crew by holding up the emerald. Recovering her breath, Jean was able to shout over the noise of the sluice box, "Here is what you are looking for!" From that day forward, in addition to her title as "the Golden Girl," Jean also became "the Emerald Girl," and she got to keep her emerald as part of her division that year.

Today, Jean Thornton likes to spend half the year in Key West. She is no longer an active diver, but her connection to Mel Fisher Expeditions still qualifies her to be considered a family member. Jean is also honored as a Key West celebrity as she rides her bike through Old Town and frequents the fabled spots where everybody knows her name. Among her local involvements, she has championed the saving of the Chart Room Bar where Mel was a legendary customer, the establishment of the Miss Loretta Medical Assistance Fund, and participation in Mel Fisher Days (2014) where she fielded a "Dream Team" of Key West Conchs to compete in The Amazing Mel Fisher Treasure Hunt. Their $100 entry fee, along with many others, went to Wesley House Family Services, a charity that benefits children and families throughout the Keys.

When her husband Joe retires, the plan is to live full time in Key West. Their investment in the future of a unique lifestyle extends beyond Jean's 18 years as a Mel Fisher Expeditions member. Jean believes that Kim and Lee Fisher are providing the leadership for a new age of discovery of which she and Joe will be a part.

Into the Blue, Secrets of the Deep

THE MAJOR EVENT DURING Division Week is a costumed gala world-class beach party at the Casa Marina, a Waldorf Astoria Hilton resort with the largest private ocean beach in Key West. The huge hotel property dates from 1920 and was the terminus of the Overseas Railway as envisioned by railroad tycoon Henry Flagler, who pioneered tourism in Florida with his railroad lines and hotels. The Casa Marina was designed to cater to the rich and glamorous, but during WWII it was taken over by the Navy to serve as officers' quarters. In 1950 it was restored as a luxury hideaway favored by such Hollywood luminaries as Gregory Peck and Rita Hayworth. Today, after another major restoration, Casa Marina thrives as a vacation destination and a meeting and convention site.

The primary responsibility for making their expedition members' gala—titled "Into the Blue, Secrets of the Deep"—the party-of-the-year in Key West falls to Sharon Drager, Marketing Manager, Jan Stauch, Finance Manager, and Shawn Cowles,

Director of Investor Relations, and Star Fisher, Inventory Manager. As if planning and supervising the seven-day events that include more than ten dinners, parties, and entertainments were not enough, the trio must outdo themselves year after year from the previous year's gala. They must somehow recreate the "wow" factor when guests arrive at the Casa Marina beach party.

An hour before the first guests were scheduled to arrive, Sharon and Jan, wearing long evening dresses, were among the 32 tables of ten tending to the place settings and supervising the staging of the final element in their centerpiece design: a two-foot tall, six-inch diameter clear glass cylinder vase with blue glass ovals on the bottom, suspended sea fans up the sides, and a live fish swimming in what could now be termed a fish tank. When carefully hand carried in by Jan's husband Ray and Sharon's husband Billy, the heavy vases that were equipped with self-illumination, had just had their live occupants added. The long carry ended when the vases were placed within a bed of orchids and delicate fern greenery at the center of each of the 32 tables, with an additional two on the buffet tables. These unique table centerpieces would have won best-in-show at decorator design shows anywhere. To acknowledge the extreme care in the handling of the live tropical fish, a formal card at each place setting requested the guest not to touch the water in the tank and not to tap on the glass. The well being of the fish was a high priority, and at 11 p.m., the event staff removed each fish for safe transport back to its own home aquarium.

In keeping with the gala theme, a private decoration firm was hired to string blue LED lights and colorful clear sea bubbles over the entire expanse of the dinner tables. The visual effect was that the dinner party was being held below the ocean's surface. A professional bandstand stage with a 50-ft. decorative backdrop and several smaller side platform stages were set up under the large lighted rectangular space, and full-service bars with top-shelf brands were available for libations. One of the bartenders, Manuel, had been employed at the Casa Marina for 24 years, and he had served every Fisher expedition member party held there.

Two long buffet tables were set up on the sand beach near the waterline. Each buffet could be accessed on both sides for a rapid service of the elegant menu that featured Key West fish, meat, and vegetable specialties. At the end of each main buffet was an individual prime-beef carving station and a separate side-standing station for the service of coffee and desserts. The dessert tables alone were objects of art that played in concert to the beautiful and bountiful buffet. Surrounded by an oceanside tropical paradise, the experience lavished all the senses.

Kim and Lee had rooms in the hotel where they would don their elaborate pirate costumes. Lee had to undergo four hours of preparation for the application of Hollywood-caliber makeup and the fitting of a curly black shoulder-length wig and full-length costume. Even people who knew Lee had to do a double take when she appeared poolside on her way to the party. She looked either like a movie star who had escaped from a movie set, or a beautiful captain's wench who had just come ashore from an anchored pirate ship.

Kim arrived at the guest entrance to the party fifteen minutes prior to its start. He was barefoot and costumed in an elaborate pirate captain's fancy silk shirt, decorative vest, and ballooned pants. An authentic sword and pistol were on his wide belt, and the total effect was capped with a rakish wide-brimmed black felt hat. Kim was all smiles as he greeted his staff and early arrival guests.

When Lee made her grand entrance and stood beside Kim, there was a scattering of applause for their striking appearance. Then Sharon escorted them to a backdrop staging area just off the main path to the dining area for photographs by a professional photographer. Couple by couple, and group by group, Kim and Lee greeted their guests and posed for pictures with all of them. The photos would be available as mementoes of the evening, but most partygoers had their own cameras, cellphone and otherwise, to document their participation. Kim and Lee were kept busy most of the night posing for photos at the individual dinner tables and elsewhere, but they did not neglect the wonders of the buffet nor the enjoyment of seeing the musical entertainments from their front-row table.

The master of ceremonies for the gala was Shawn Cowles, the Investor Relations Director, who spent the entire night on dry-wall installer stilts wearing a very elaborate flowing blue sea creature costume. From previous exposure at Division Week events, one could easily imagine that Shawn was making a personal appearance from a nationally televised game show. His personality is that large. This same guy, you must know, was a dive supervisor for the Army Corps of Engineers and a member of the U.S. Deep Wreck Diving Team, who has explored the ocean bottom at depths of up to 300 feet using mixed gas and closed-circuit technology. In 1994, while diving on the *Atocha* and *Santa Margarita* shipwrecks, he and his shipmates recovered 96 emeralds during that season. So if you get caught up in Shawn's fun-loving nature and comedic talents and pose for photos with him, just remember that in the world of diving for shipwreck treasure, he has "been there, done that."

The live entertainment for the party began with a gifted female singer during the dinner hour and then continued with a colorful and unusual group that seemed to be a jazz-folk fusion band. During a band break, a featured solo act stopped all table conversation and focused eyes on the main stage. The young woman in the bikini was the world champion pole dancer, and she was a gymnastic marvel. It was quickly rumored that pole gymnastics might soon become an Olympic sport. One could believe it from her performance. It was not so much erotic as it was Cirque du Soleil, a pole suspended contortionist's defiance of gravity.

One of the highlights of the Division Week Saturday night party is the costume contest. The winner at this year's event received a Grade One *Atocha* coin valued at $2800. Although many guests opted for elegant tropical party attire, most of the revelers were in elaborate costumes. Apart from the costume shop rentals, some of the costumes had been custom designed and fabricated over a period of weeks if not months. For the guests who created their own costumes, it was not the prize so

Photo by Mel Fisher's Treasures

*Michael Piscotty and Esther Knapicius won the
2014 Division Week gala costume contest.*

much as it was the competition that motivated them. Where else but Key West, a town crazy for costumed events, can such creativity be recognized?

The 2014 costume winners were Michael Piscotty and Esther Knapicius from Parkesburg, Pennsylvania. Michael is an audiologist, and Esther is a mental health service administrator. They have been expedition members for 17 seasons, a commitment matched only by Jean Thornton, who is known as the Golden Girl *Atocha* Diver around Key West.

At any Division Week gala, Michael and Esther have to be considered amongst the favorites to win the costume contest. In previous years, Michael had won as an exotic bird and again as a deserted guy on an island. Last year, an inconvenient illness took him out of the competition, so for 2014, he and Esther went all-out to win. Their winning concept and personal craftsmanship took about 80 hours of detailed labor. The fabric alone for their giant "Seahorse named Margarita" had to be matched at three separate fabric shops. No one place had enough yardage.

When completed, Michael carefully put on the wire-framed body of the 9-foot-long seahorse whose head and snout ranged several feet beyond his own. His screened viewing portal was in the creature's neck. The large tail of the seahorse stretched out behind him, as Esther was required to lead him through the groups of fellow guests. The winning gimmick of the costume came when Esther invited people to "feed" Margarita small simulated gold brick ingots. The ingots were styrofoam that had to be primed, painted, and applied with gold glitter in a very long five-step process. When the gold bricks were put into the seahorse's mouth, flashing lights and dancing movements indicated that Margarita was "digesting" the gold. Then, as the giant seahorse turned away, "she" pooped out "good luck *Atocha* coins," which some young people scrambled to collect. Their winning costume edged out a handmade deep-sea diving suit with helmet that was constructed by last year's winner. Michael and Esther donated Margarita, the Seahorse, to the Fishers to be auctioned off in a charity fundraiser. Last seen, Margarita was hovering in the company headquarters break room, waiting to be claimed.

José "Papo" Garcia: Captain of the M/V Dare

THE HISTORY OF KEY WEST is intertwined with Cuba, whose local fishermen crossed the 90-mile Straits of Florida in colonial times to trade their goods with the locals in Key West. Today, the historical port has become the Old Town Tourist Center with streets still lined with the original bricks used as ballast on the arriving ships. As the arriving ships unloaded their ballast of bricks for trade and sale, the ship's load was lightened, thus allowing room for freshly acquired cargo for their return voyage home.

Havana, as one of the most populated colonial cities of Spain's New World empire, was the assembly port for treasure ships. Here the ships from the different routes would rendezvous, provision, and prepare for their three-month voyage back to Spain. During their stay in Havana, the ships would complete any repairs, load their provisions, prepare their manifests, observe the weather, and organize the fleet to sail.

The route across the Atlantic required the Spanish galleons to negotiate the treacherous Florida Straits where many treasure-laden galleons met their fate. Passing south of the Florida Keys, and east of the mainland, they would maintain their northern heading, riding the Gulf Stream until they reached the 36 degrees of latitude that would provide them a direct line of crossing to their destination in Cadiz, Spain. The fortunes of many generations of people who inhabited Cuba and the Florida Keys thus became intertwined by this trade route of Spain and by the hurricanes that scattered shipwrecks along its reefs.

When Cuban Navy diver José "Papo" Garcia ended his military term of service, he was allowed to continue his occupation with a government-owned underwater salvage company named CARISUV. There were no private companies in Fidel Castro's Cuba. The estimated number of shipwrecks around Cuba and the Southern Caribbean in the 1980s was something around 2,000. During Papo's diving years with CARISUV, the government-owned company found nearly 100 of them. One treasure wreck dated at 1500, which pre-dated the *Atocha* (1622), produced gold bars, silver coins, and small cannons.

Over the years, Papo increased his proficiency as a commercial diver and also was schooled in underwater photography. His expertise in marine archaeology was recognized to the extent that Papo was selected by the Cuban government to represent it at professional conferences. During an official tour in 1996 that included a conference in Texas and weeks at the National Geographic Society in Washington, D.C., Papo made a stop in Key West for the purpose of meeting Mel Fisher and learning more about his salvage operations. Papo had a lot to share because he had also worked with salvage companies around the world, and he had participated in dives with the French on sites in Egypt and the Philippines. Mel was impressed with Papo's gregarious personality as well as his professional accomplishments.

Back in Cuba, restrictive social changes were occurring that affected every business operation, including CARISUV. By 1999, it became a common practice to force otherwise civilian-led companies to accept retired military men into their leadership ranks. The companies thus became controlled by Castro's military arm. This disruption led to the financial failure of CARISUV within two years, but Papo had already decided to immigrate to the United States. And although Mel Fisher was no longer alive, Papo was welcomed by the Fisher company when he arrived in Key West in 2000.

Papo had to wait for two months to get his immigration paperwork done, but then he was hired immediately to work on one of the salvage vessels in the boat yard. When company leaders became more aware of Papo's extensive professional résumé, he was soon moved to the crew of the M/V *Magruder*. During 2003 and 2004, Papo also worked in the conservation laboratory and on the archaeological database with company vice president Gary Randolph. Then in 2005, he became the captain of one of the two major salvage vessels in the Fisher company fleet.

Papo's crew on the *Dare* is mostly Cuban, so you might expect the galley, especially, to reflect their tastes. When the groceries are brought on board for a ten-day trip to sea, the big bags of rice and black beans are prominent. It is said that Papo likes to do a lot of the cooking himself. The main crew meal of the day, by ethnic custom, must therefore feature a meat or fish served with white rice, black beans, and sweet plantains. The meats may vary from chicken, sausage, shredded beef or steak, roasted pork, or pork chops that have been flavored with a sofrito spice mixture. The classic sofrito consists of onion, green pepper, garlic, oregano and ground pepper quick fried in olive oil. There are always tortillas and very strong coffee to complement a Cuban menu. A good after-dinner cigar seems appropriate, too.

During 2013 and 2014, the *Dare* underwent a refitting and inboard redesign to accommodate the development of the *Dolores*, the ultimate underwater search and survey vehicle. The *Dare's* salon took on the look of a NASA flight control center with its many consoles and monitoring screens, and Gary Randolph with his elite technicians worked on the main deck to prepare *Dolores* for her sea trials. With Papo and his crew in support, the trials were run, and the *Dolores* was made ready for a season of deep-water explorations.

Between sessions in support of *Dolores*, the *Dare* continued its ongoing salvage mission. In October 2014, Captain Papo and his *Dare* crew were working in deep mud on the *Atocha* site. The mud work is difficult and time consuming for the divers, but the mud itself protects artifacts from oxygenated seawater and keeps them relatively safe from storm erosions. What the divers recovered on this fall day was an ornate hardwood bedpost that company conservators and archaeologists believe to be part of the *Atocha's* cargo.

The tall bedpost appeared just as new as when it was shipped in 1622. It has no wear on the bottom, and its shape is still nicely rounded and without any scratches. The speculation is that it was commissioned by a wealthy merchant, a member of the Spanish nobility, or by a senior member of the Catholic clergy. It was probably made in the New World in either Cuba or South America for shipment back to the buyer's Spanish homeland. Because the bedpost was found near the main pile of the *Atocha* wreck site, the hope is that this discovery will lead to other fascinating artifacts from the same cargo hold.

Photo by Mel Fisher's Treasures

Papo displays the rare bedpost recovered in 2014.

The conservation of the unique bedpost presented a challenge to company conservator John Corcoran. The porous and organic nature of wooden artifacts from 17th century shipwrecks makes their survival very rare. To arrest disintegration, the bedpost was put into a custom-built conservation tank with salt water. The salinity of the solution will be gradually decreased until all the salt has been removed from the wood. That initial process alone is estimated to take a full year. Meanwhile, the meticulous job of removing the concretions by dental picks will proceed.

One of the most interesting aspects of entering the treasure salvor's world is the characters that you meet. Especially on the boats, you will encounter adventurers who would have joined crews in any age of discovery. There is something restless and daring in the DNA of their makeup. Mostly, they cannot find the words to describe themselves. They are instinctual in this regard. They prefer direct action to the passivity of other possibilities. When you meet José "Papo" Garcia, Captain of the *M/V Dare*, you are shaking hands with a long line of Spanish explorers who will pass through him into a future of even greater discoveries. We know more about the moon than we do about the depths of our own planetary oceans. That gap is closing steadily by men who sail on ships like the *M/V Dare* and the *JB Magruder*.

Headed Back to Sea

MOST OF US WHO HAVE submerged ourselves into the treasure salvage exploits of the Fisher company have done so vicariously. Maybe we have actually dived on the *Atocha* Mother Lode site, or even acquired an Emerald City gemstone, but few of us have ever had the experience of being a crewmember on board the *JB Magruder* or the *Dare*. If we applied for crew status to work the 2015 season, what would that life be like?

When you interview for a place on the salvage boat crew, you need to show your scuba diver certification and convince Captain Andy Matroci or Captain José "Papo" Garcia that you have a solid work ethic and that you possess the maturity, character, and personality to fit in with the rest of the crew. You will also be asked if you can cook.

The crewmembers of today are much older than in the 1970s and 1980s. There are a few men in their 20s, but the range tends toward 40. The Captain, himself, is nearer 60. If you are not yet settled in Key West, you can live on the boat, but the captains know that you need a break from shipboard life, so they encourage you to have a personal one ashore. Your accommodation on board is in a crew cabin below decks where you're assigned a bunk bed and a storage compartment. Both the *JB Magruder* and the *Dare* have air-conditioning, so there is that comfort.

Your captain wants your boat to be able to go to sea on short notice as the weather dictates, so soon after the boat is docked, a fuel truck is called to pump diesel into its two tanks. On the *JB Magruder*, each tank holds 3,000 gallons. The amount of fuel taken may be anywhere from 1,500 to 2,500 gallons depending on the planned days at sea and its movements back and forth from night anchorages in the Marquesas to avoid choppy seas. There is fresh water at the dock, so the boat tops off its water tanks with 7,000 gallons.

There are always dock-time work projects to occupy the usual four-man crew. There is chipping and painting, attention to the dive gear, and general ship maintenance. It is summertime, and the captain announces that the boat will soon depart for ten nights at sea. For the crewmembers, that means meal planning and shopping for all ten days. The captain pays for the groceries out of his working fund.

You've been told that you rotate with your three other crewmembers in the cooking, serving, and galley clean up of the main nightly meal. Breakfasts and lunches of leftovers and deli foods are self-serve, mainly because daylight operations and dive turns do not stop for meals. As the new guy, everyone wants to know what you like to cook. Pork chops? Meatloaf? Italian pasta with shrimp? Well, not to worry. There are cookbooks in the galley. You will learn. You have also noticed that the captain is not on the cook's roster. In ten nights at sea, you, as the low man in the deck crew, may have to cook and clean up at least three times!

Well, you can't be as bad as one newcomer who began to cook for his first time on the *JB Magruder*. Andy was at the wheel headed for a Marquesas night anchorage when the boat's mate told him that he had to come to the galley to see the new guy trying to make mashed potatoes. The untrained cook was dutifully, aggressively, trying to mash the peeled potatoes in a bowl, but they would not mash. He was then advised that he probably ought to boil the potatoes first. The poor fellow lasted years with the crew and became an acceptable cook, but his bout with the mashed potatoes is a favorite *Magruder* sea story that often comes to the surface.

While all other meals on the working boat at sea are catch-as-catch-can, the evening main meal is served and eaten as a family gathering. The meal is served after the boat is anchored for the night. If the boat has made an hour's run to seek shelter for the night in the Marquesas, the food has been cooked en route, and the meal is served soon after anchoring. The men plate up in the galley and either eat around that table or take their plates and beverages outside on deck.

Wherever the food is eaten, it is eaten together. Now there is time to share and discuss the events of their day and to speculate on the work of tomorrow. Now is the hour for joke telling, personal reminiscences, and lies about one's love life. Now comes the bonding that molds a crew into an effective and efficient salvage team. Comradeship also multiplies the margins of safety in a sometimes-dangerous occupation. You must know that you can count on each other whenever circumstances turn against you.

Because you are new on the boat, you may wonder about Captain Andy when you catch him silently staring at the chart table for fifteen minutes at a time. Don't bother him, you are told. He's cogitating in a kind of intense meditation that has led to treasure before. The charts have lots of plot lines and markers for where treasure has already been found. They mark trails that Andy knows so well. There is now, of course, all that same information available on the pilothouse computer, but this captain likes the feel of paper charts and the glow of the light table that adds a degree of mysticism to the decision process. Anybody who has ever found shipwreck treasure will tell you that intuition, informed or otherwise, plays a big role in success.

When Andy first became one of Mel's captains and had a personal relationship with him, he would report to the salvage company office with his sea charts to discuss a recommended search area. The decision was important because it would commit the boat and the company resources for the next four to six weeks of working in that same area. Andy remembers Mel as the great motivator who placed much trust in the judgments of his captains. When Kim asked Andy to return to the company to command the *JB Magruder*, Andy reported to the office with his sea charts to plot a new search area. Kim told Andy that he had both the knowledge and the experience to make his own search area decisions. Thereafter, Andy came to the company office to get his boat's payroll, not for salvage instructions. For a boat captain, being trusted to hire your own crew and work your own plan is the best possible environment for success at sea. On February 1st, 2015, Andy celebrated the 13th anniversary of his *Magruder* captaincy.

One of the basic things that you have to learn as the new guy is the primary importance of the boat's generators. There are two of them—a day genny and a night genny—each rated at 30 kilowatts. Everything runs off those generators. Everything electrical and everything mechanical. Generators power the wheelhouse hydraulics for steerage. They power the deck wenches and the pumps for the toilets and the sinks. If one of your generators goes down, you cease operations and return to the dock. The old adage is, "one is none, and two is one."

You also quickly learn that your cellphone will not work once you are more than 10 miles from Key West. The boat has two VHF radios—one for marine use and the other to make contact with the company office. There is a large antenna atop the Greene Street Museum building to facilitate contact with the boats. The boat captain also has a satellite phone for emergency use, but the minutes are too costly for personal calls. Crewmembers will not be calling their wives or sweethearts on this phone. And frankly, captains dislike hearing it ring. It always seems to bring bad news.

You have stayed busy on your three to four-hour run to the search coordinates, but now the real work begins. The captain has located the buoys that mark the locations of the three one to two-ton mooring anchors that the boat positioned on a previous trip. To set or reposition the three huge mooring anchors with their chains takes two to four hours of hard, skilled labor. Fortunately for you, it won't be done today.

Your boat has towed a work skiff with a 150-h.p. outboard engine, and now the 21-foot skiff is brought alongside and loaded with a line to be connected to one of the mooring anchors. The chain ends are then shackled together in order to stand the great stress that is to come. When all three lines are connected, the *Magruder*, for example, is anchored by a bow anchor and two stern anchors angled behind the boat, port and starboard. Each anchor line is 1200 feet long, and when they are winched tight, the salvage boat is fixed into position and very stable with regard to wind or tide.

Perhaps the most ingenious aspect of the anchoring is that the boat can be maneuvered by loosening one line and tightening another, like a spider adjusting itself on a web. The boat needs to move only about 15 to 25 feet in a desired direction to reposition itself for the mailboxes to make an additional hole in the sand. This method allows for the prop wash excavation of as many as seven to nine holes in a diving day. And if you have to make a run to the Marquesas for an overnight-protected anchorage, you can return the next day, reconnect to the three mooring anchors, and get quickly back to the prime time of putting divers into the water at a specific location

The new guy is already fatigued by handling the heavy anchor lines, but now attention turns to the lowering of the two mailboxes. Your boat has already been fitted with 12-foot metal cages welded to the hull that cover the twin propellers. The cages are both for the protection of the propellers themselves and for the safety of the divers. Some earlier mailboxes had elbow-end cages that fit over the props. Once their locking travel pins have been removed, the 2000-pound each mailboxes are lowered by electric wench into the water, and a diver descends to place a stainless steel pin on each side of the mailboxes to lock it into position, securing them to the hull of the vessel. Unexpected swells can interrupt this process and result in the boxes banging uncontrolled against the hull of the ship, which is extremely dangerous for the diver trying to secure the boxes to the hull while he/she, too, is being pushed around by the surging waters.

Once the diver is back on deck, the boat's twin engines (three on the *Dare*) engage the propellers, and seawater is directed down the mailboxes toward the floor. Each engine is a 12-71V diesel with 12 large cylinders that generate 475 h.p. The force of the propelled water excavates a deep hole in the sand that spans

15 to 25 feet across consisting of exposed hard pan surrounded by 6 to 12 feet high walls of sand. The ocean bottom is thus exposed, and any artifacts that are there can be seen or found on the floor or in the side sands of the hole.

The dive order for the day has been previously determined. The senior divers usually take the first rotation. A designated "bottom" diver goes to the bottom of the hole with a metal detector and begins to do a circle search. A circle search consists of starting in the center of the hole with a metal detector in one hand and eyes opened wide, sweeping left 3 feet swaths and right 3 feet, covering 6 feet of the floor as he/she swims around the center of the hole. With each completed lap, the diver moves out 6 feet from the center and repeats until the entire 25 feet of the floor has been checked. His fellow diver has been assigned to work the sand walls in a similar fashion from the top of the wall to the bottom. This keeps the divers separated and prevents their detectors from "talking." If two detectors come close to each other, they interface signals and give a false reading.

The captain is more concerned about thoroughness than he is about speed. A diver has enough air in his tank and bottom time to search two holes if the depth is not too great. The boat captain does not put himself in the dive rotation, but he may join his working divers to observe conditions or to offer further training. After each rotation, divers refill their scuba tanks at the compressor on deck.

There is one fundamental credo that your boat captain constantly reinforces. Whatever you do at the dock or on the deck at sea, you do it for only one reason: "bottom time." Finding treasure is a direct function of "bottom time." You keep yourself fit and sacrifice your personal life for the sake of "bottom time."

So you got your first "splash," but you have no idea of what was required by so many people to put you there. The excitement of possibly finding gold on your first dive floods back memories of how it felt as a child on Christmas morning. Many folks experience beginner's luck and surface with a ballast stone or perhaps a pretty shell. Now back on the surface, you frown in the disappointment of finding nothing. Maybe you notice your more experienced shipmates shaking their heads at your naiveté. How many holes did they have to work until they found something of value? Hundreds? Time to take a break on deck as the next dive team goes into the water. As the adrenaline subsides, you may notice you are feeling both hungry and thirsty; this job requires a lot of energy. As you finish a quick lunch, another realization occurs—you can't wait to get back into the water. The next hole may be the fabled sterncastle, the next Mother Lode, with history once again being made, and you could be part of it.

Part of your crew training and professional orientation to shipwreck salvaging is learning the archaeological and conservation protocols of handling the treasure itself. In your excitement of finding an artifact in the sand, whether it be a cannonball or a silver plate, you have to pause and remember that an important part of your job is to document your underwater discoveries in situ so that the archaeologists can interpret it. Some of your new skills will be operating an airlift to expose the varied artifacts. You may also become adept at carrying out the three-dimensional survey of a wreck site.

When your artifacts come on deck, the captain will record them and give them an identification number that will stay with them throughout perpetuity. Then the conservation process needs to begin immediately. Most artifacts that you recover from the seawater need stabilization to counteract almost 400 years of salt being absorbed into the material or reacting with the silver, creating a silver sulfide concretion. The boat is equipped with saltwater tanks on deck to serve as the initial conservation process. Even gold, which is impervious to the elements, will be submerged in water. All these details and much more will become familiar to you.

When you were hired, you were told that expedition members in the company would come on board to dive with you while you were working a hole. They would be accompanied by a dive master, but your job description includes helping them with their dive gear and seeing them safely up and down the diver ladder. The member guests would be taxied to the boat around 9 a.m. and depart around 4 p.m. There would be six of them at a time, both men and women. Be courteous. Be polite. These guests underwrite your paydays. During the day, you will come to know and appreciate many of them. Make them welcome. Give them a great experience that they will always remember. It's to your advantage. Members often arrive with luck on their side, and they find treasures while working at your side.

The *JB Magruder* is now the primary boat that anchors over the Emerald City site so that members can work the sluice boxes in search of emeralds. You may be required to work the airlift below that pumps the bottom materials into the boxes. The excitement, however, occurs on deck as emeralds are found, and the screams of joy are mixed with the clang of the ship's bell. The *Magruder* will host up to ten member guests a day during its annual three-week stay on the Emerald City site. Emerald City was so named because every trip to that site produces emeralds. The company has reason to believe there was a 70-pound chest of Muzo emeralds being smuggled on the *Atocha*, and to date, less than 6 pounds have been recovered.

When fuel and groceries run short, or the weather turns against you, you prepare for the four-hour run back to Key West. Captain Andy likes to work a full day, anchor overnight, and then make the run to port early the next morning. Andy has created 8 x 10 laminated sheets for every department on the boat. You don't have to guess what to do. There is an instructional list for everything. On the way in, there is a clean-the-boat drill that lasts about an hour and a half. You may be recovering lines, bagging the garbage, or washing down the decks with a fresh-water fire hose. This is no sunset cruise.

The run in from the ocean through the Keys is through deep channels, so you don't worry about ship traffic until you approach Key West. The entrance into the marina, however, is tricky. Yachts and other pricy boats line the waterway, and running the gauntlet between them provides only two feet of clearance on each side. It was okay when you left port because you always depart in good weather, but the return weather can be very different. Bad weather sometimes drives you back to port, so there you are, struggling in the wind. And if you are on the steel-hull *Magruder*, you can do a lot of damage to wooden and fiberglass boats by scraping along their hulls. But, all is well. Your boat turns in the inner marina and ties up at its docking space after pointing itself back to sea.

You've got your return-to-dock cleanup and maintenance assignments to complete before your workday ends. Tomorrow is another workday because your captain wants the boat made ready to return to sea. Finally, you get two consecutive days off from the boat, and if you are lucky, it's the weekend. When bad weather keeps your boat at the dock, you work an 8-to-4 schedule, with an hour off for lunch, five days a week. These are the days to defrost the refrigerator and freezer, change the engine oil, and perform the repairs and maintenance jobs on your captain's list. These are also laundry days.

Your crew position on the salvage boat is salaried. You don't punch a clock to get paid by the hour. You are counted as an independent contractor, and you are responsible for your own taxes and insurance. You are taking the risk that your boat will be the one to find the next great treasure and that you will share wealthily in its division.

If you pass the tests of your captain, shipmates, and the sea, then you will have earned "bragging rights for a lifetime," and perhaps one day you, too, may take your child or grandchild to a maritime museum and point to some very rare and valuable artifacts in a display case and share your stories. Such is the life of a treasure hunter.

About the Author

Photo by Shawn Cowles

Like his father and grandfather before him, Monty Joynes was raised on the Chesapeake Bay of Virginia where boating, fishing, and crabbing were a lifestyle. At age 16, he spent a summer as the third cook on a Norwegian coal freighter that passed through fog banks and a stormy North Sea to make ports in Europe. He returned to Europe on a freighter after taking a degree at the University of Virginia and was later drafted into the Vietnam War-era Army.

In literature, Monty is regarded as a pioneer author in the Visionary Fiction genre with his five Booker Series novels. His 20th book, *Confessions of a Channeler*, was published in 2014. Monty also has authored feature film screenplays and classical music libretti in adaptations from his novels. His published work includes another two-subject biography, *Journey for the One: The Biography of Jeanne White Eagle and John Pehrson* (2008). He is also the award-winning author of military combat short fiction.

Monty and his editor-partner wife Pat live in the high country of the Blue Ridge Mountains of North Carolina. They have three daughters and ten grandchildren.

To learn more about the literature of Monty Joynes, visit his website:

http://www.montyjoynes.com and blog,

http://www.writingasaprofession.wordpress.com